"My mother and father raised me, but Olubode taught me how to, think, shift and bloom. During the formative years of my career his coaching and mentorship created a powerful environment to test and examine my modern ambitions and be held accountable, while balancing the spiritual scaffolding of my parents and ancestors. With his guidance my chaotic mindset was unearthed and a new type of thinking emerged. I am successful because of it. That foundation orders my world and informs my decisions every day." ~ **Erika Alexander** – Actor, Activist & Producer

"Olu's words activate that which already resides in each of us, answers to the question: 'What is Life asking of me?' This book is an answer to a collective sacred prayer. It holds gifts that we need, right now." ~ **Kinshasa Carvalho**

"Olubode is the twenty-first century go-to person for artists who want to realize their creative possibility. As a composer and creator of digital content for film, television, recording, and the Internet, whenever I am faced with a problem that I don't understand, I rely on him to listen intently and to ask the questions that get me moving. He is a powerful mix of creativity, business, and spirituality. His counsel has helped me to move forward boldly, and continuously." ~ **Patrick Gandy** – Composer

"This journey was my path to personal and professional transformation, healing, and purposeful life mapping. This process of self-discovery and renewal helped me to find my true voice and essential self in a

meaningful dance of light and shadow, by boldly facing and faithfully embracing all parts of myself – my essence and my desires – in ways that empowered, ennobled, and energized my dreams, goals, and desires for myself and the world around me. It was simply a mystical experience."
~ **Tyrone Fitzgerald** – Attorney-at-Law

"*This journey has been incredibly fruitful for me. Writing felt like rest — my desk actually became a place of rest and simplicity. I have never ever experienced anything like that. This program is tough; it's a lot to think about. But I feel it was really critical to getting my work done and doing it in a way that I can imagine doing for a lifetime — I can imagine actually having a partner and a family because my work doesn't have to make my life chaotic.*" ~ **TF** – Writer & College Professor

"*This program has given me the tools to keep myself clear, focused, and productive. It was well worth the time spent.*" ~ **Malcolm-Jamal Warner** – Actor/Director

"*For those of us who are often overwhelmed by professional and personal responsibilities, Olubode's system is a godsend. It helped me define the real priorities in my life and organize my workday accordingly.*"
~ **Lisa Jones** – Author/Screenwriter

"*Olubode's work on passion projects and finding your essence really inspires me. One workshop with him and the lessons have lasted a lifetime. After 10 years, I still refer to the booklet on Essences... I can't wait for this book to come out!*" ~ **Andrea Dempster Chung** – CEO Go Global Art

BLOOM

THE ESSENTIAL JOURNEY

Mizuri,
Earth moment!
You are the
ground on which
we walk! Truly
Thank You for
us all!
Oliu.
11/2017

BLOOM

THE ESSENTIAL JOURNEY

A New Guide to Balance, Growth and Well Being

OLUBODE SHAWN BROWN

BANYAN TREE PRESS
New York City

© Banyan Tree Worldwide Media, Inc. 2017
Published by:
    Banyan Tree Press
    445 W 125th Street
    New York, NY 10027
    212-749-5891

Interior layout and design by www.writingnights.org
Illustrations by Demeree Douglas and Olubode Shawn Brown
Cover design by Olubode Shawn Brown
Book preparation by Chad Robertson and Olubode Shawn Brown

ISBN 978-0-9903058-0-4

Book Website
www.theessentialjourney.com

Printed in the United States of America
Printed on acid-free paper

24   23   22   21   20   19   18   178   7   6   5   4   3   2   1

DEDICATION

To my ancestors whose dreams I carry,
to my mother who held my hand to teach me how to write,
to my father who taught me to dance,
to Malidoma Somé and the Dagara of Burkina Faso who helped
me
remember,
to all my teachers, too many to list
I lay this gift at your feet.

The Nature of this Flower is to Bloom

Rebellious Living.

Against the Elemental Crush.

A Song of Color

Blooming

For Deserving Eyes.

Blooming Gloriously

For its Self

~ Alice Walker

CONTENTS

ACKNOWLEDGMENTS

This book arrives at the confluence of many streams, embodied in amazing friendships, family, community and business partnerships. I call their names here as a testimony to their contributions and with great gratitude. ***Andrea Dempster***, the midwife of this book. She saw me struggle towards the finish and came with her coaching, management skills and resources to gently and firmly see to its birth. ***Ronald Myers***, whose friendship, belief and generosity gave me the time and space to focus. ***Robert Clarke***, my brother, for his love, guidance and companionship during the long night. ***Orin Saunders*** and ***Kelly Peterson***, who have been the keepers of our memories and watched over me as these ideas unfolded for over 20 years. **Ann Denise Brown**, my sister, who has always loved and supported me, even if we did not always agree. **Sharon Campbell**, who has always had my back, and **Kaneil Murrary**, a steadfast steward of our resources. Together at BLOOM Central both Sharon and Kaneil were patient and supportive as I focused on writing this book in the face of our financial perils. ***Andre Palmer***, whose daily reading of the manuscript during a period of critical writing in Jamaica pointed to gaps to be filled and reminded me of the power of acknowledgment. ***Tama Smith***, whose strategic mind insisted that I prioritize this book and the production of *The Essence Cards* above all else. ***G.***

Winston James, my editor, for his diligence and patience through each phase of editing. *Deborah Huisken,* whose edits during the final phases of writing proved critical. *The Seedlings—Neila Ebanks, Kinshasa Carvalho, Robert Clarke, Donovan Manning*—and the members of *Transformation Jamaica,* who created a home in Jamaica for these ideas. *Landmark Education, Devorah Gilbert* and the members of the *International Black Summit,* who saw me before I had eyes to see myself. My brothers from *Other Countries*—living and deceased—who first acknowledged my voice and listened to my stories. The *Agape International Center of Truth* in Los Angeles and *Rev. Michael Bernard Beckwith,* whose teaching and guidance are a constant affirmation. Each *Backer* who supported this project financially with their contributions and belief, without which this book would not be here now. To **BLOOMERS** around the world with whom I have prayed, partied, dreamed and worked, thank you for opening your hearts and giving me a home. Finally, *Randy, Robbie, Andre* and *Adaku,* my Suns, who each day help me to find my sense of direction. Keep shining brightly.

INTRODUCTION

"There is a vitality, a life force, an energy, a quickening that is translated through you into action, and because there is only one of you in all of time, this expression is unique. And if you block it, it will never exist through any other medium and it will be lost. The world will not have it. It is not your business to determine how good it is, nor how valuable, nor how it compares with other expressions. It is your business to keep it yours clearly and directly, to keep the channel open. You do not even have to believe in yourself or your work. You have to keep yourself open and aware to the urges that motivate you. Keep the channel open."

~ MARTHA GRAHAM, RENOWNED CHOREOGRAPHER

MY NAME IS OLUBODE. For over 25 years I have been an attorney and life coach. Today, I am the facilitator of a global movement called BLOOM.

It all started nine years ago when we created a New York City dance party called BLOOM. Since then, BLOOM has grown with regular events in New York City and a yearly freedom festival in Jamaica for people who have resolved to be free. Today, BLOOM is evolving as a community of people who are creating new ways of being in the world for our own survival. I call us BLOOMERS and I have written this book for us so that together we can keep ourselves well and growing as we deliver some amazing gifts to the planet.

What we are discovering about balanced growth and well-being is what I share in this book. The systems and philosophies outlined here are the foundation on which BLOOM is built. It is a book about our humanity and the urgency of delivering the powerful gifts we each have for the world.

At stake are our health, well-being, and gifts that are urgently needed.

Perhaps you are a BLOOMER too.

Ask yourself the following questions:

- ☐ Are you wanting to take the next step, but with no clear path ahead you find yourself facing off with self-doubt—the fear that you will not be understood, heard, or thought to be relevant?
- ☐ Are you fearful of the changes that taking, or not taking, the next steps will bring—feelings like not being in control on the one hand, or of feeling stuck on the other?
- ☐ Do you want to work at what you love and be seen and rewarded for that, yet fear that folks will not get it, or get you for that matter?
- ☐ Do you want to have a strong team yet are wary of the feelings of isolation and abandonment that often result from personal conflicts and sudden departures?
- ☐ Do you want to create a lifestyle in which you have it all, yet fear you will not be able to manage it all?

These dynamics present a balancing act that too often pits our health and well-being on the one hand against the special gifts that we each have, on the other.

BLOOMERS are:

1. Creative and social entrepreneurs.
2. People who are juggling jobs as they create their own enterprises.
3. People with stressful careers who are seeking to be more productive while bringing greater balance to the ways they live and work.

Can you relate to any of the above? If you can, you are a BLOOMER too.

I can relate. I have been there and am right there with you now. In my life-coaching practice, in countless seminars and encounters I have journeyed far with people who are BLOOMING. With each person, we have been on a journey to find what really matters to us because we are each balancing multiple projects and modern lives with all of their compartments, desires, fears, unpredictability, speed, and societal demands.

This book is the story of our shared journey and the discoveries made thus far along the way; insights about what really matters and how to use that knowledge to keep balanced, deliver our gifts, and bloom.

I invite you to take this essential journey with me now.

AS WE ENGAGE MORE CHALLENGING PROJECTS and ideas about our life's possibility, each day brings us to *a crossroad.* We are brought there, up-ended perhaps by the chaos of things—difficult relationships, regrets about the choices we have made, the stress of not having enough resources, or a sense of having too little time to do all that we really want to do for ourselves and our communities. These crossroads are transformative opportunities for us to locate within and without, a new sense of balance—a fluid center that moves in tandem with the unrelenting urge to grow in self-awareness and accomplishment.

Currently we are moving towards the tipping point where more of us are beginning to remember our connection to the natural world and our essential goodness. We are arriving on the planet with multiple and seemingly divergent gifts at a time when the technologies with which to communicate these gifts are pervasive. Increasingly too, we have begun to make bold choices to pursue these diverse and seemingly discordant passions with authenticity. In so doing, we are challenging the ways we identify ourselves, do business, create art, build communities, organize politically, love, parent, and spend our time.

We are creating alternative social structures that allow for unique self-expression, personal growth, visibility, connection, and belonging. This is a movement of BLOOMERS—**global citizens who are finding innovative ways of responding to the evolutionary changes of our time for our own survival.**

This book seeks to inform, inspire, and celebrate this movement, as too often we are delivering our gifts at the expense of the things that matter most: our well-being, close relationships, community, family, and fun.

Today, we are surrounded by a culture in which we are charged with balancing so much on an impossible scale. Half of that scale, we have been told, should hold our "personal life" and the other our "work life." This misguided way of thinking pits work against living, and divides the personal from the professional as though they are in fact separate and equal; as though we somehow come to our workplaces as different people than we are. We have been programmed to believe that the viability of everything that's called a "personal life" is based on the success of what is meant by "work." This deception implicitly asks us to sacrifice our well-being, leisure, passions, relationships, and community building if we are to achieve "success," yet sets us up to be too stressed to enjoy that achievement.

This dynamic jeopardizes the next stage of our human evolution.

Now more than ever, the gifts we bring to the planet are urgently needed. The desires and projects that challenge us, though uniquely ours, are not just a personal phenomenon. Every new idea that truly inspires us holds the future of the entire planet in its potential, not only because these are great ideas, but because the process of their manifestation transforms us all.

You and your dreams are one. As you are being transformed by the birthing of your ideas, you transform us all. The path to personal and planetary evolution is unfolding through each of us causing us all to see ourselves in new ways.

The world needs all of our gifts, ideas, and unique self-expression to energize our organizations, families, and communities. Indeed, we have seen awesome gifts unfold, but consider that some of the greatest life altering ideas were stillborn and are now waiting to be resurrected. These ideas died because the individuals through whom they came buried them out of fear; because the people brought together to realize them did not get along; because someone insisted on having it their way. Oftentimes we think that the goal is only the destination and not also a path that will personally transform everyone involved and thereby change our world.

To manifest these ideas, individuals, communities, organizations, teams, and families must take a courageous journey into themselves to discover more of who and what they really are, why life brought them together, and the gifts they have for each other. This book provides such an opportunity.

Together we have the resources and the talents to enjoy as much prosperity as we can imagine, but first we must decide to walk together. We must help each other to find our unique and essential selves and desires, unmasked from our individual and collective survival strategies; to see clearly the magnetic power of a shared vision; to receive our warriors—the difficult people in our circles—as gifts; and to re-learn how to take care of ourselves individually and collectively in our circles of engagement.

This is the essential journey of living. Being challenged in delivering our gifts is simply an opportunity to journey even deeper into expanded self-awareness, to find new and hidden centers of power and balance from within and without. The purpose of this book is to share new ideas to help us to do just that—to find new centers of balance from within and connect them powerfully to what we do and can accomplish in our human lives. This book is for us when the urgency to deliver <u>ALL</u> of our life's gifts has become unbearable.

א When we can hear the call to a new and unique path for our lives that promises even greater well-being and personal fulfillment;

א When we are ready to have a renewed sense of adventure about living;

א When we want to make a greater difference on the planet by doing what we love and to be acknowledged and valued for that commitment;

א When we are ready to build new personal and working relationships that are authentic, deeply connected, and creative;

א When we are building a community that nurtures and receives everyone's gifts and talents.

In the process of birthing my own dreams and midwifing the gifts of others, I have noticed the emergence of a paradigm from which a new life balancing equation can be extracted. This new framework is emerging from the natural world. This world offers an exciting way of identifying the basic elements that keep all things balanced. This paradigm has been hiding in plain sight, obscured by our material focus. Yet, it offers us the possibility of a more sustainable and non-self-destructive pathway to balancing our modern lives and delivering our gifts.

This new model connects our inner and outer lives and in so doing transforms the old dualistic social framework of "work-life balance"—that artificial divide that now underpins much of our current dysfunction. As a culture, we are working more hours with more

technology and an overflow of information, yet we are not more fulfilled. We work for five days, but are only really productive for three,
yet we experience less time to do the things that really matter to us.

If we continue operating within this faulty framing we will not
be able to respond well to the desperate need for innovation. We will
not be able to keep our economies and communities fresh and vital.
Stress related illnesses will continue to rise, family connections will
continue to disintegrate, and our unique gifts will be lost to the ma-
chines that our modern lives now mimic.

This book offers a solution. Its purpose is to make the hidden
natural paradigm of life balance clearly visible and to encourage us to
use it to create a new social culture that provokes the full expression
of each of our special gifts.

Using as metaphors the five elements: mineral, nature, fire, water, and earth—the elements that grow and transform all living
things, I will introduce you to:

I.   The **five essential life-nutrients** that balance and grow our
      lives. This natural hierarchy of needs is the true basis of our
      psychological health and personal growth. *Our desire to ex-*
      perience these life-nutrients constantly drives ALL human
      behavior. I will show how our externalized quest for them—
      a unique dance between our goals and our hidden fears—can
      keep us stuck. We will learn how to break free by under-
      standing the deeper nature of our desires and the distinctive
      patterns of behavior we manifest because of the fears to
      which we are each vulnerable.

II. Next, as a challenge to the current dualistic framing of "work" versus "personal life" balance I will introduce us to the five life-areas in which ALL human beings have activities. I will explain why we often over-do activities in each area at the expense of our well-being. I will further show how to use each of these five life-areas as ritual spaces to refresh our connection to each of the five life-nutrients. In so doing our experience of fulfillment and productivity will increase in every area of our lives.

III. After this, I will introduce **25 new personality archetypes.** These archetypes are inspired by *Masharishi Mahesh Yogi's* codification of the qualities of the unified field as outlined in **Deepak Chopra's** book, *Creating Affluence.* For me, they are also the qualities of LOVE, and we are its embodiment. Over time, I have observed that these 25 qualities also describe the activity of each of the five elements and of our own essential nature, and that these qualities express as fundamental aspects of our personalities in varying degrees. To demonstrate how this happens, I will introduce *the* **Essence Cards.** This deck of 25 cards describes each of the 25 distinct human personality archetypes—both their light and dark sides. In them, I will show you how to identify the three that now best describe you, but which become shadows of themselves—your worse qualities—when you are stressed due to the specific emotional fears to which you are vulnerable. Also in the deck are the three essences that you have desired. You will learn how to put your specific personality archetypes together to create a new and dynamic way of understanding your unique human journey.

IV. Next, we will meet **the five dragon-fears at the *crossroads of life*** to which we are each uniquely vulnerable. These are the fears encountered most often in the course of delivering our gifts and in our relationships with our tribe—the people closest to us. These individuals include the difficult ones who push our buttons, people who are family, co-workers, playmates, community members, and political allies. Using the five elements I will reintroduce us to each other and help us discover the vital roles we each play and the unique gifts we have for one another.

V. Finally, I will put it all together by sharing a starter kit: a template, with which to design powerful nature-based rituals to help integrate the specific fears to which we are each vulnerable. I will also introduce an energetic roadmap of our inner nature. This will give us a new way of understanding our bodies and its five energy centers that are connected to each of the five elements. Combining our awareness of our outer and inner natures will create a powerful conduit for balanced growth, well-being, and ultimately the full delivery of our gifts.

This book is presented as stories and insights from my own journey, as well as conversations from my journey with clients who are personified here as Madra. Along the way, there will be meaningful, insight-inducing exercises to engage us. Each exercise is represented by a GUIDEPOST.

A guidepost indicates a place where questions are asked or a practice suggested. It is recommended that you pause and engage each exercise as completely as you can. Reading further without doing so will make this book a purely mental exercise. Whereas when completed, each exercise will help increase our self-awareness and develop important life skills for growing our sense of balance and accomplishment.

Some exercises will challenge you to engage your emotions honestly. You don't have to get things perfectly the first time you do an exercise. Your insights and answers from working with this material will expand and deepen over time. Some of you might find it best to do these exercises with a close, trusted group of friends or advisors. However, once you've started the process of asking the questions presented in these exercises, the answers and insights will begin to work in you whether you are conscious of it or not. Because each exercise builds on the others in previous chapters, this will be particularly true if you continue to practice the contemplative tools in earlier chapters.

In much of this book, I have chosen to use the pronoun "we" to remind you that I am also on this journey with you. The exceptions are when "you" is used to communicate more directly to you --for emphasis, or where the use of "we" is unexpected and obviously awkward.

Finally, I promise that if we take to heart the ideas in this book they will change the way we now think about our lives and what is possible for us—our families, our work, and communities. It is my hope that this journey together will catalyze insights that will change all our lives for the better as we respond to the next stage of our human evolution.

Olubode Shawn Brown
Kingston, Jamaica

PROLOGUE

"The Soul of the World tests everything that was learned along the way. It does this so that we can, in addition to realizing our dreams, master the lessons we've learned as we've moved toward that dream... the darkest hour of the night [comes] just before the dawn."

~ EXCERPT FROM: "THE ALCHEMIST" BY PAULO COELHO

I REMEMBER THAT NIGHT lying in bed and panicking at what I imagined might unfold from writing this book. With each thought, I shuddered inwardly, worrying that I would not be an exemplary model of its principles and that there would be no place to hide.

How humiliating, I thought, that just before I could complete it, I would become a lunatic in my efforts and a shameful example of hubris. *How dare you tell folks they can balance it all when you can't? What have I gotten myself into now?* In the wee hours of the morning these thoughts flooded my mind as I neared what I thought then was the end of writing.

I had just returned to my apartment in New York City after three years of being away. Between a failed relationship and an impossible one, I needed a place to belong. I had many things to prove, and as yet few results to show. After twelve years of promising everyone a book about my work and setting a date for its delivery, there would be nothing to show. Just when it had all been figured out, I began to fall apart.

Old wounds had begun to resurface.

I remember stumbling out of bed to my yoga mat, stretching my body for a bit then climbing onto my meditation chair. There I steadied myself with several long slow breaths before the first clear thought came.

"You are at the crossroads," I heard.

The realization made me smile nervously.

It wasn't long after that first clear thought that another one came: that an insight into all these doubts and insecurities must be in the very book I am writing. Quickly, I lifted my phone from the edge of my chair and opened it to the journal entry I had written earlier that day. It was a draft of a passage for this book.

There I read these words:

> *"More than just a choice of direction, a crossroad is an opportunity to become. It is there that you must gently embrace the fears of irrelevance, hopelessness, invisibility, loneliness, rejection, and chaos. You must surrender all images born of these fears and reach in deeper to greet like a long-lost friend the essence of your becoming ... amplify its quiet insistent vibration, let it pour out of your wounded spaces and become one with it."*

I was not to escape having written these words without putting them more deeply to the test. That morning I sat still and allowed myself to feel every physical sensation in my body. I felt each wave of emotion. I heard every thought debating my impending demise, saw the images, and felt the heat they generated. Yet, beyond all that I was aware that a fluid source more powerful than those thoughts was alive *as* me. This sense grew stronger as I remained focused on it.

As the sun rose, I was at it again, writing with more joy, clarity, and compassion—feeling more alive as I placed each word on the page.

Chapter I

The Challenge of Balancing It All

"And the day came when the pain of staying tight in the bud

was more painful than the risk it took to blossom."

~ Anais Nin

Meet Madra

MADRA, A WRITER AND ASPIRING PRODUCER, met with me over lunch on New York's Upper West side. During our meal, she talked about her "baby"—the web series that would, in her words, "revolutionize the media landscape." This was the idea that had finally turned her on while holding out the promise of providing so much for so many. It would enable her to work full-time at something she truly loved. According to her, it would transform an *ad hoc* mixture of part-time gigs and far-flung enterprises into a purposeful adventure. She glowed and spoke of its possibility in both reverential and guilt-ridden tones. One could not help but sense her creativity, dynamism, and imagination. We connected easily. Yet, to hear her tell it, she was always starting over.

She had begun and stopped working on her idea several times over the last five years—never seeming to "have all the right pieces."

"I have had so many dreams shelved and, honestly, I have to give life to them or I will either burst or shrivel in regret. Dramatic I know, but I do not want them to die inside of me unrealized. They are meant for the world and my next step has to be to garner help for their delivery. I know in my heart and gut that this journey will help me deliver it."

"What do you think is missing?" I asked her.

"I don't know" she said, *"I am juggling so many things and working all the time, but this is something I must do."*

We spent the afternoon chatting freely—getting to know each other and arranging a series of calls for us to accompany each other for a while on our journey.

Before we parted I placed in her hands a colorful deck of 25 cards and asked her to choose the three cards that best describe the way she knew herself—the ways she couldn't help but be, for better or worse.

Each one of us, regardless of our present level of accomplishment has a big dream that challenges us deeply. Most of us have had our idea for a long time. For many of us, like Madra, in the course of holding down work, managing a home and raising a family, or running a business, such a project or gift can get lost. Periods of rapid expansion or inertia may have left us with a sense of being overwhelmed, unbalanced, and unfocused. Although we may be accomplishing different things we feel that we are repeating the same experiences over and over again.

Yet through it all, like Madra, we hold on to these ideas not just because they will do good for so many, but because at a deep level we suspect they fulfill our basic drives to be heard, to thrive, to be seen, to connect, and be at home.

This is why our dreams matter to us—dreams about the health we want to have, relationships we want to enjoy, work we want to create, adventures we want to pursue, and the kind of businesses and communities we want to build.

In the landscape of our minds, these ideas are like active volcanoes, erupting from time to time, then lying dormant for long periods. We may forget our ideas for a while, but they remember us. With each eruption comes feelings of anxiety, guilt, or shame for not having done enough to make them happen. Somehow, we feel that we are not ready regardless of knowing we are not complete unless we act on these projects.

So why then do we procrastinate?

In James Baldwin's letter to his young nephew, published in his collection of essays, ***The Fire Next Time***, he writes:

> *"People find it difficult to act on what they know. Because to act is to be committed, and to be committed is to be in danger. In this case, the danger is the loss of your identity. Try to imagine how you would feel if you woke up one morning to find the sun shining and all*

the stars aflame. You would be frightened because it is
out of the order of nature. Any upheaval in the universe
is terrifying because it so profoundly attacks one's sense
of one's own reality."

In short, we procrastinate—give excuses, sell-out, and take measured steps in sync with the *status quo* of things—because to do otherwise would up-end our current identity. What little sense of control we have over our lives and any sense of balance we can now imagine under our present cultural and personal paradigm would be in jeopardy. To act without knowing "how to" and without guaranteed success and acceptance is a frightening challenge.

When we act in new ways, in search of a new experience, how we see ourselves and the world will be unalterably and unpredictably changed. This is the root of all procrastination—fear of the loss of our identity precipitated by an upheaval of the behavioral structures and familiar circumstances that now keep us secure. This upheaval will place in jeopardy the comfort of our current relationships. We may face rejection, confront hopelessness, run the risk of not being heard or understood, and/or make embarrassing mistakes. Yet it is in the process of delivering our gifts that life's most essential journey takes place. It is there that we will be challenged to reclaim our authentic voice, learn to respond courageously to chaotic change, see and value ourselves more clearly, experience a profound connection to others, and experience an abiding sense of belonging.

In these ways, our ideas and dreams that call for new action are the harbingers of our personal deconstruction and the evolution of our identity and our world.

Along with all that, the new center of balance we crave will come. But seldom, if ever, do we get up in the morning and say, "Oh, I want to balance my life." Instead here is a list of the types of things we actually say:

- א "I am not being heard. I am just going to shut up or shout louder!"
- א "Things are not moving fast enough or too fast. I need to get away or control things."
- א "They don't really see me. I am being disrespected."
- א "What is wrong with them? What am I doing wrong?"
- א They don't want me here. I don't feel safe here."

Which ones have you been saying?

Whenever we catch ourselves thinking in these ways there is an opportunity to step into a new identity—to BLOOM—to find a new center of balance and power from which to move forward.

Finding new centers of balance is the prerequisite to continued growth. All living things require a unique balance of essential nutrients. If not found at each phase, growth becomes stunted or deformed. **Finding balance is what matters.** To find new balance we must be courageous because the current social culture—based on an old formula of life balance—offers no possibility for the life we envision for ourselves.

THE IMPOSSIBLE EQUATION

EVERY SO OFTEN the issue of "work-life balance" raises its head in the media and folks, including former First *Lady Michelle Obama,* take a stab at addressing the concern by commenting on our need for balance. Famously, Anne-Marie Slaughter—the Director of Policy and Planning at the State Department under Hillary Rodham Clinton—created a stir when she was quoted in *The Atlantic* saying, "Contrary to what we have been led to believe, women who work and have families still can't have it all." Men also argue that they are feeling the competing demands of work versus home as much as, or even more than, women, given our culture's expectations of men. So, no one is having it all—not inside the current problematic framing where work and personal life are offered as the only two spaces human beings inhabit, and in which the word "life" is used as a catch-all phrase that is the opposite of "work;" whereas in reality life includes work, and so much more.

Yet our material culture with its focus on capital creation charges us with balancing these two separate ideas—work as the counter-weight to life; one being better than the other depending on your place in the social order of things: one in which workers try to do less and business owners strive to extract more from those same workers.

In truth, we also have family businesses, social enterprises, creative entrepreneurial ventures, and not-for-profit organizations in which business, family, communal and social lives all have to be juggled in the same field of activity. Beyond those engagements there are political justice issues that we care about, friends we love but seldom see, religious or spiritual communities, and a host of other important concerns that go unattended. There are books we want to read that might help us grow that sit on shelves unread; new creative passions that remain unexpressed; and the nagging need to take care of our bodies and emotional health that is continually neglected. When we are able to energize these seemingly external concerns though, something in us opens and new creativity is engaged, enhancing our mental, physical, and social health as well as the enterprises we are so focused upon.

For too many, our lives have become a complex set of floating balls to be juggled while new elements are being thrown into the mix constantly. Under the current limiting framing of work-life balance we do trade-offs: over-doing work at the expense of our health, or opting for more leisure at the expense of viable work or sustainable working habits. For example, you may say, "I'll work hard for the next three years so that later I can have some fun and then I'll have a family," or vice versa. But then everything changes. You fall in love, get laid-off, get divorced. Taking care of your health or that of aging parents becomes necessary or you develop new passions. Trade-offs assume that we are in control of all the variables life can throw our way. But this is not how life happens. Life seems to give us everything it can throw at us and in ways that are unpredictable and constant. Yet, we seem hardwired to try to have it all by latching onto choice bits and pieces that we think will balance it all.

Compounding our dilemmas is the fact that more and more technology and gadgets are being sold to us ostensibly to help us manage our modern-day lives. This technology promises us the things we crave: to be seen, heard, stay connected, take control of the future, and ultimately bring order to our lives—all at a faster pace and with less effort. These days there's an app for everything—ones to help us keep up to date with our to-do lists, record our favorite shows, and get us home faster.

To add even more complexity to the equation of "life balance" is the fact that we have more information at our fingertips than previous generations. With this information overload, we can literally "learn" about almost anything online. As a result, today we are more likely to pursue multiple interests that challenge our need for stability on the one hand and the desire to follow our passions by doing innovative work, on the other.

Whether we are men or women working in a suite of corporate offices, working moms juggling two jobs, or fathers needing to spend more time with their families; whether we own our own businesses or are executives or leaders of not-for profits trying to figure out how to make our staff more innovative; whether we are un-employed or artists making our way in the world; whether we live in an inner city and are struggling to meet the most basic necessities, or high flying ballers, we are all on this journey to find new centers of balance that will help us deliver our gifts to the world and to live more productive and fulfilled lives.

Like the art of juggling, life balance has fundamental natural mechanics that can be learned, practiced and mastered. However, it can only be done well when ALL the fundamental internal and external elements of the life balancing equation are known.

Currently, we only have bits and pieces of the equation dispersed over many disciplines. To achieve equilibrium in our lives we must have a complete set of basics from which to improvise, knowing that the fundamental elements that nurture all our lives are the same, regardless of gender, age, profession, geography, or race.

What are the fundamental elements of this life balancing equation? Where do we find them and why do they matter?

This we will discover in the next chapter. But before we do, let's get ready for the journey by setting some goals.

SETTING YOUR GOALS FOR THIS JOURNEY

SOON YOU WILL BE ASKED TO SET GOALS for this journey. My request is that you include at least one goal around completing a project that delivers your gift to others.

We all have a gift to deliver to the world. The delivery of this gift is our life's purpose. But understand this: there is the gift we have, and then there is the gift we give. The gift we give is the one that we created with the gift we already had. So for example, we may have the gift of singing, but our gift to the world is a song. Our purpose in this life is to deliver the best and most impactful song we can sing.

Each gift is as unique as we each are. Yet, we often wonder what our gifts are and how to deliver them.

The Path of Passion

I HAVE COME TO SEE that there is a path of passion that leads us to realize our gift and purpose. Following our path of passion simply means doing what we love. By "doing" I don't mean we have to pursue it immediately as our work. For some of us doing that with immediate action and dedication may be possible and appropriate. For others, though, "doing" may be realized as an expression of our play/leisure, or as something that supports our well-being, home, family life, or as a contribution to a community or group.

Often our passions will direct us to areas in which we may not have any expertise or knowledge or into areas where our emotional vulnerabilities will be exposed. The road won't always be comfortable. That's okay. **Getting on the path of passion and navigating its twist and turns is the first step to finding new centers of balance from which we can grow afresh since navigating it will require us to be balanced in ways in which we are unaccustomed.** Albert Einstein once said, *"Life is like riding a bicycle. To keep yourself balanced, you have to keep moving forward."*

Our passions define the roads we will navigate on this essential journey.

All of our passions are interconnected and support each other in ways that we may not be able to currently see. Our passions are energies, each with varying levels of intensity. They are layered and we often have to fully mine one layer completely before another emerges. Sometimes one passion pops out of another spontaneously. Passion is a pointer of direction. It is not static, it moves around. Passion leads us to one idea, then to others and then strings them all together to help us realize the gifts that we have and to help us create those we will give to others. It is passion that opens the way and connects the dots, so follow it.

At one point it my life, I no longer wanted to coach and I was burnt out on living in New York City. At the invitation of my friend, Orin—also a great coach and facilitator—I stayed at his home in Charlotte, North Carolina. I just hung out with him for 6 months. It was a tremendous gift. In the mornings, we would have these great conversations. During one of our first conversations he asked me, "What do you really love to do?" I answered, *"I am passionate about putting together great parties."* Orin grinned widely, *"Yes you do, and you have!"*

"I love bringing people together, but to be truthful I also do it in part because I don't like feeling alone or stuck—a great party makes me feel like things are moving along and we are all in it together... So should I not follow that passion because I am just a lonely guy trying to find company?" I asked.

Sagely he advised, *"Keep throwing them because that will lead you to the other things that you also love."*

And it has. It was out of my love for producing parties that BLOOM first emerged. Over time I saw that I am also passionate about connecting us all in meaningful ways, and that my own life experience gave me a deeper compassion for others and an understanding of our need to connect. This led me to ask, "How can I help us all to connect more deeply?" It is by following the path of this passion, asking that question, and contributing my answers to others that the idea of BLOOM continues to evolve to help us make more meaningful connections with each other *and* within ourselves. Following my path of passion--though a flight from pain, has allowed me to bring together my talents and all the things I love—art, photography, writing, insightful conversations, travel, spirituality, great friends, and fun.

Our passions connect our wounds—the places where we are in pain—with our best qualities and talents, then folds them into a wonderful gift in which everyone can partake.

GUIDEPOST 1.
DO THIS NOW
Keep asking yourself:

✗ *What are the things that I am really passionate about now?*

✗ *What are the gifts and talents I have been given?*

✗ *What do people really want and need?*

✗ *Given my passion and the gifts I have been given, what can I provide for others?*

I found the following quote recently. I love its bluntness.

"The common complaint among a lot of people is that they need to 'find their passion.'…You already found your passion; you're just ignoring it. Seriously, you're awake 16 hours a day, what the […] do you do with your time? You're doing something, obviously. You're talking about something. There's some topic or activity or idea that dominates a significant amount of your free time, your conversations, your web browsing, and it dominates them without you consciously pursuing it or looking for it. It's right there in front of you; you're just avoiding it. For whatever reason, you're avoiding it. You're telling yourself, 'Oh well, yeah, I

love comic books but that doesn't count. You can't make money with comic books.'.... have you even tried?"

~ MARK MANSON

So, in setting your goal for this journey first follow the path of your passion.

Second, make a project of it and commit to it. If you can, first do it as a fun project—as an adventure. **A project is a specific and measurable EXPERIENCE that you want to have NOW and also have PHYSICALLY MANIFEST at a time in the future.** Make it a B.I.G.—BIG IMPOSSIBLE GOAL. You don't need to know how you will accomplish it. It is through our passion projects that we "*re*-member" - put ourselves back together in this dimension. We do this by surrendering to our paths of passion and committing to produce a result without knowing completely how. It's in the gap of not knowing, the emptiness of this dilemma that we BECOME. This becoming unfolds new joy, freedom, power, and the new balance that we are really after.

Here are some signposts that will help you know if you are on the right track to discovering and delivering your gift now:

1. You don't know how, but you have decided to take the next step

2. As you pursue your goals, the way you see yourself and the world is changing

3. You have had to become more visible in order to deliver your gift

4. You can sense that it will not be possible for you to accomplish your goals alone

5. Your life is expanding, and you now have to find new ways to manage it all

GUIDEPOST 2.
DO THIS NOW

In a journal write down the three BIG goals that you want to accomplish in your life right now, even if you have previously felt hindered in accomplishing them. For each goal, write down the challenges: what stops you or slows you down and why. It could be a thought, a feeling, a person, or a circumstance. Before moving on to the next chapter, take some time to make the list as truthful and complete as possible.

Also, as you read and gain insights from this book, your project and its goals may change and deepen. This is okay. Simply notice the change and make the necessary adjustments in direction. Keep each goal in mind and use the ideas shared to help you move forward.

Keep moving forward!

CHAPTER II

THE NEW LIFE BALANCE

"People given any destination can, depending on what is available, choose to go there by bike, choose to walk there, run or fly there.

For the Dagara people, my people, what we choose as means of transport to get down to that essence [of life] is what the natural world is offering."

~ MALIDOMA SOME

WHEN I WAS ABOUT SEVEN YEARS old in Jamaica I learned how to ride a bike. My friend, Winston, tried to teach me. He was thirteen at the time. It was on a grown man's bike with down-handles that Winston had pieced together from scrapped parts. The gear control lever popped out of a small handmade wooden box below the cross bar. I would sit on the cross bar and Winston would sit high on the seat behind me and let me steer and pedal while he covered my small hands with his.

I trusted Winston, but I was terrified.

We crashed several times.

Winston introduced me to a bike, what it is and how it works, but to learn to balance on one I had to take it out for a spin by myself several times, crashing into the pump at the local gas station, braving traffic, falling and gouging my knees. But with mastering its use, a whole new world opened for me.

Since then bicycles haven't fundamentally changed. There are newer models on the market with better parts and lighter frames, that enable us to go faster and farther, doing things never before imagined. But the basic model remains the same. Neither has life changed despite seeming to—with all the new technology, scientific discoveries, gadgets and information we now have. What has been missing for us as navigators of our own lives is a deeper understanding and mastery of the basic model of life and living.

In attempting to balance life, we as a culture are crashing as I did with Winston on those roads in Kingston.

Let me be your Winston. Let us go on a journey together with a new model of life balance.

Like riding a bike, with practice you will eventually begin to get the hang of it. I will show you an updated apparatus—a new approach that I believe will open new possibilities for all human beings. It will provide a new way of seeing life, one that will help us see more of the fundamental aspects of what is being balanced.

We will take it out for a ride. I will show you where the pedals are, how to work the brakes, suggest when to change gears. I will also introduce some inner skills that we can build on to accelerate our learning and focus our attention where it is needed most.

After that, you can take this new model of life balance out for a spin by yourself. You will learn naturally how to sit on the seat and how to move your weight around to find your own center of gravity. Eventually, we will learn other new tricks like riding side saddled, with our feet on the handlebars, over tight ropes, and mountains. Soon we will add our own unique flavor to things until the way we each ride becomes our unique self-expression. I hope together we will invent new ways to ride that are going to change for the better the way we all work, play, engage family, and take care of our personal and communal well-being.

First let's lay a foundation for life balance with an introduction to its basic elements.

THE FIVE ELEMENTS OF LIFE BALANCE

"What is this thing with the elements?"

Madra's question, though anticipated at some point, seemed to come out of the blue.

"Are you suggesting that I need to spend more time in nature?" she asked.

"No, I am not saying to go sit in a garden, at least not yet," I responded.

"The elements are written all over the cards you gave me, and I was just wondering about their significance. Is this some kind of 'voodoo' thing?"

I could hear her humor and the concern in her voice so I took her question seriously.

"What if these elements could help you see a new way to move things along, would you be willing to try to understand how they work?" I asked.

"I would," she replied tentatively.

"Then let me tell you a bit about them, how my interest in these elements started."

With that exchange, I explained that many years ago an elder man from Nigeria came up to me and gave me a new name. He called me Olubode. It's a Yoruba name from West Africa. Loosely translated it means the "keeper of the sacred garden." The name my parents gave me is Shawn Brown. But his naming of me on a street corner in Brooklyn took naming to a whole other level and started me on a journey to discover the personal significance of that name. In that pursuit, I found my life's mission—to provide spaces that inform, inspire, and celebrate our human journey.

Later I studied and worked with Malidoma Somé who introduced me to the five elements that comprise the world-view of his people. Malidoma is an initiated elder of the Dagara people of West Africa. He helped me understand how his people use the five elements to keep themselves well. For the Dagara these elements—mineral, nature, fire, water, and earth—are necessary to bring balance and growth to individual and communal life. This world-view comports with many indigenous traditions around the world. Eastern thought and Ayurveda had intrigued me for some time, so I recognized this worldview as a truth echoed by Vedic Rishis—the wise men of India—who declared:

> *"Out of Brahma, [which is the Higher Self] came space; out of space came air; out of air, fire; out of fire, water; out of water, earth; out of earth… the body of all humanity"*

> — TAITTRIYA UPANISHAD

Though the words used were different, the energies to which these two ancient cultures speak and their sequencing are the same. Mineral and "Space" (in some traditions called "metal" or "ether") are the same element, as both are symbols for an energy found within the core of the hardest substances known to man, yet ethereal enough to be known as "Space." Both hold memory. Similarly, NATURE and "air" point to the same element, because all that the Dagara knew as NATURE—the plants and animals—breathed air.

What did these seemingly distant cultures know that had them utter the same truth? They seemed to know the same truths reflected in the cultural and spiritual traditions of the people of ancient Egypt, Greek philosophers, the Yoruba of West Africa, and the Asiatic peoples. What they all knew was a simple truth: that everything in life expresses these elements and that the well-being of human beings and the planet rest on the inner and outer balance of these five elements.

Here are the symbols for each of the five elements that will be used throughout this book.

MINERAL   NATURE   FIRE   WATER   EARTH

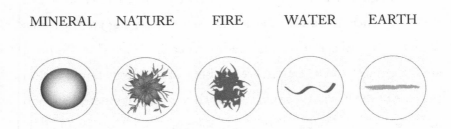

The Elements

ALL GROWING THINGS NEED THESE five simple things —mineral, nature, fire, water and earth. Observing plants will tell you this. These same elements are at work in the cosmos supporting all life. They are responsible for growing things and for sustaining all life on our planet. Our deepened insight into the alchemy of these elements has powered important leaps in our evolution as a species: the discovery of fire to cook, the planting of the first crops, the creation of tools from stone and metals, and the demystification of the laws of aerodynamics.

What if these elements are also metaphors for everyday activities, and decoding them can help us understand how to more consciously participate in the balanced evolution of our humanity and culture? If their presence is required for all things to grow, what then can these same elements tell us about the next stage of our *inner* evolution? Because of my study and work with people like Madra, who are trying to accomplish challenging personal projects while living modern lives, I have had the chance to observe how these elements when used as metaphors can in fact help us see into the inner and outer workings of our lives. They are able to tell us something more about who we are, about how to better balance our lives, and bloom, by being more productive and innovative in sharing our gifts.

Let's take a closer look at each of these elements.

Mineral

MINERAL is the element that helps all living things to progress and to remember. It is the element that activates the internal blueprint present in seeds. It promotes the healthy development of fetuses in the womb. This is the element that gives all living things their unique beauty and appearance, and contains everything needed to activate us fully. It is symbolized by stones and bones in the Dagara culture. Other traditions refer to it as metal, space, or ether. Each reference points to substances that hold memory and information and give us stories about who we are. This element speaks to the part of us that seeks to give voice to ourselves as singularities— unique, unrepeatable expressions of a whole. Mineral is a way of knowing things, as in when someone says, *"I can feel it in my bones."* It is symbolized by the color white.

Nature

NATURE is the second element. It is encapsulated by all things that utilize air for their subsistence and vitality. Some traditions call this element "air." It is a metaphor for change, transformation, and inter-action—the attributes of all growing things. It allows for harmony, adventure, spontaneity, and freedom. It is an element that knows no boundaries. Nature is the home of all we encounter on a walk through the outdoors—freedom, spontaneity, and the orderly cycle of life. It is symbolized by the color green.

Fire

FIRE is the element that allows for inner and outer vision and cre-ativity. It is the element of exchange: the place where ideas are born, imagined, created, and shared with others. It is the element of man-ifestation. It conveys fundamentals from the invisible side of life into the realm of the visible. Fire purifies and makes things invincible. It is the house of commerce, work, and creativity. It is symbolized by the color red.

Water

WATER is the element that connects, nourishes, and touches all living things. It speaks to that part of us that wants to find peace, reconciliation, and empathy with others. It is the reason our attitudes become more peaceful when we are near streams, lakes, rivers, and the ocean. Water connects us all emotionally and allows for compassion, clarity, and self-sufficiency. It is symbolized by the color blue.

Earth

EARTH is a metaphor for order, stability, safety, nurture, and support. This is not earth in the conventional sense of referring to the planet Earth. It refers to the ground and soil in which things are grown. Earth is the element that allows for community, giving, fertility, power, belonging, and order. It is symbolized by the color yellow.

In the following chapters, I will use these elements to help us to identify:

- ℵ The five essential life-nutrients—inner psychological pillars that are needed to balance and grow our sense of fulfillment and accomplishment.

א   The five life-areas in which ALL human beings are active.

א   The 25 human personality archetypes as derived from the five elements.

א   The five dragon-fears at the crossroads of our lives that threaten to keep us stuck, unable to deliver our full package of gifts, as well as ritual practices needed to break free of those fears.

Here we go!

CHAPTER III

THE FIVE THINGS THAT REALLY MATTER

"So, what would you say is stopping you or slowing you down from moving forward with your project?" I asked Madra.

"It's a number of things. My project is a bit strange and people have odd ways of relating to it. There are just soooo many pieces to it that have to come together and everyone has an idea about how to do it. Also, to be truthful, I feel stuck at times. I am not really sure how to move forward. I wish I had more contacts and resources to really pull this off in the way I see it. I want for it to be done well. There is just so much that's out there that just looks bad!"

She paused. She had exhausted herself, but I sensed she was on a roll.

"What else is stopping you now?" I probed.

"My team keeps changing," she continued.

"Everyone is busy working on their own projects. When they do

help, I have to wait on their timing. No one has time to work with me to start something that is not going to pay at this point. I don't have the money to pay them to pull this off…and, these are people whose projects I have worked on."

I listened intently with my ears tuned to the familiar ways in which we lose balance as we unfold our ideas.

Beneath Madra's answers (and most answers to this question of what is stopping you or slowing your down) is a search for what I have come to recognize as the five things that all human beings MUST have. We need them like plants need minerals, earth, sunlight, air, and water to grow. I call them the "essential life-nutrients." They are why things bloom. They fuel everything, including our projects. Having these life-nutrients is the key to delivering our gifts. Yet it is only when we actively engage our ideas that these life-nutrients are found. One could say that the reason we have ideas and dreams is to launch us on a quest to find the life-nutrients we need.

Madra, without knowing, spoke about her quest for these life-nutrients. She mentioned:

1. Needing to **HEAR** and sustain her unique **VOICE** through this project
2. Her feeling that things are not **CHANGING** quickly enough, coupled with a loss of **HOPE** and a feeling of being stuck
3. Wanting to be **VISIBLE** in ways that best represent her
4. The frustration of not feeling **CONNECTED** or supported by the people around her

5. Not feeling **SAFE** or viable given her present circum-
    stances, resources, and contacts.

Madra's project represented her unique path to finding and expressing her connection to life's essential nutrients.

What are these nutrients?

THE FIVE LIFE-NUTRIENTS

The five elements: MINERAL, NATURE, FIRE, WATER, and
EARTH are metaphors for these five essential life-nutrients we
ALL crave. They are:

1. VOICE
2. HOPE
3. VISIBILITY
4. CONNECTION
5. BELONGING

These are the psychological pillars that allow us to remember our
uniqueness and express it, enjoy the adventure of change, feel valuable, create fluid teamwork, and authentic relationships that build
powerful communities.

When we are disconnected from any of these nutrients we:

1. Overdo activities and negatively impact our well-being.
2. Develop behaviors that compensate for the lack we feel.

These behaviors negatively affect our ability to deliver our gifts.

Later on, you will see more clearly how this happens. For now, let's take a closer look at each life-nutrient.

Here are the life-nutrients listed with their elemental correlates.

MINERAL　　NATURE　　FIRE　　WATER　　EARTH

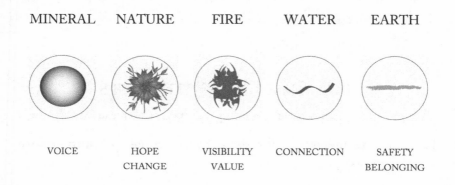

VOICE　　HOPE　　VISIBILITY　　CONNECTION　　SAFETY
　　　　CHANGE　　VALUE　　　　　　　BELONGING

The Elements & Life-Nutrients

#1. VOICE

MINERAL

The strength of our voice is the truest indicator of our overall well-being. MINERAL is a metaphor for the life-nutrient that activates our stories and memories. Voice tells us who we are. Having an authentic voice means we can hear ourselves—sense how unique and special we are—and express that identity in the world. Voice satisfies our need to be heard for the unique points of view that we have to offer, the stories we have to share, and the unique gifts we have to give. It is the nutrient that helps us remember the narrative that we use to make sense of everything. If we cannot hear the story of who we are, if we don't have an experience of having our story heard or understood, we can become silently malicious and strategic or aggressively loud and demanding. When we are deprived of this nutrient we tend to dwell on asking, "how, why and what if," and weighing the pros and cons of things to figure out the best and worst case scenarios without truly moving forward.

#2. HOPE & CHANGE

NATURE

We tend to want and advocate for change only to the extent that we possess the hope and confidence that change will not obliterate our known identities. Nature is the nutrient that allows us to negotiate and survive change. This is the nutrient that gives us the courage to move forward in the face of the unknown. Nature is always evolving and unbounded, yet it remains the same in its capacity to survive its own change. It is the element that expands our ideas about who we are in order to embrace personal change. We, as human beings, need to share Nature's confidence that though things are in flux we are able to thrive through change. We need to feel that we can challenge existing norms and create new experiences for ourselves and see new possibilities with each other. If not we begin to feel stuck and hopeless - becoming resigned and cynical or unruly outlaws. When we are disconnected from this nutrient we tend to dwell in the future or the past, unable to see the unfolding present moment. We will say to others, "I feel stuck," or "this should not be happening." We want to be anywhere but in the present moment.

#3. VISIBILITY

FIRE

As you value yourself more deeply you will see others more clearly. Fire allows us to be visible in order to see and value ourselves. It also helps us to see others and accept them as they are. This life-nutrient helps us to give and receive acknowledgement and validation to and from others. Each of us needs to be seen and accepted as our whole selves—our light and shadows. If we feel rejected or worthless, we will often feel ashamed and hide our gifts and brilliance or perpetuate a false image of ourselves and our accomplishments in order to gain acceptance and validation. When we are deprived of this life-nutrient we are not able to see beyond the surface of things. We dwell on fixing others and ourselves because we cannot see the beauty in things the way they are.

#4. CONNECTION

WATER

Because of its calming effect, Water is a metaphor for our need to be peacefully related to others. This is the life-nutrient that allows us to connect with our inner "SELF" and that "SELF" within others. It supports our ability to empathize and to act compassionately towards others and ourselves. It is the life-nutrient that engenders abundance, authenticity, and intimacy in relationships. When we are deprived of this life-nutrient we feel abandoned and will separate ourselves from others, harboring judgments about who is right or wrong. We are unable to accept the choices of others. As a result of this experience of abandonment and isolation, we can become hoarders and cold loners or needy in our relationships.

#5. SAFETY & BELONGING

EARTH

Earth is a metaphor for our basic need for safety and belonging. This is the life-nutrient that gives us the ability to provide order, nurture, nourishment and consistency for ourselves and others. It is the most basic of our needs. It encompasses our need for food and shelter as well as our need to feel at home in the world. When we are deprived of this life-nutrient we tend to complain that someone is doing something to us that makes us feel unsafe and victimized. As a result, one can become aggressively protective of one's sense of family and community, and self-sacrificing to the point of martyrdom.

HOW WE WERE DISCONNECTED FROM OUR NUTRIENT SOURCE

THE NEED TO RECONNECT to these life-nutrients and to express them naturally in their fullness during our human journey is our great quest. When we are successful in so doing, these life-nutrients un-block the internal channel through which our ideas, new levels of insight, and actions emerge and manifest.

The things that matter to us are:

- ℵ Hearing ourselves and being heard
- ℵ The hope that we will have the power to create, experience, and survive change
- ℵ Seeing ourselves and being valued for who we are.
- ℵ Feeling connected to an inner source and to the people around us.
- ℵ Feeling at home in our bodies and safe in our surroundings.

Finding and strengthening our connection to these life-giving nutri-ents *is* what matters.

We are like seeds that must be tended if we are to express our promise. When we are connected to these life-nutrients we display our full human possibilities through our gifts, talents, and our experience of ourselves. But too often we are disconnected from these vital nutrients.

This disconnection happens when the social culture into which we are born diminishes us by dishonoring our natural abilities: our ability to hear and see ourselves, to feel a deepening capacity to experience change, to be connected with all living things, and to feel at home in the world. To the extent that the culture we are born and raised in is unaware of who we really are, we will be disconnected from these vital life-nutrients by people who have been charged with our care but who are often themselves not conscious of their own disconnection and lack of self-care.

This sense of disconnection is first experienced as children and often continues through to adulthood:

- א When we are implicitly (if not explicitly) told to be quiet we lose VOICE
- א When we are told that things will not CHANGE for us, we lose HOPE
- א When we are ignored and not valued or seen, we lose VISIBILITY
- א When we are emotionally or physically abandoned or betrayed we lose the experience of CONNEC-TION
- א When we are not physically protected or find ourselves without community, we lose BELONGING

As children, by performing externalized behaviors for which temporary rewards are given, we take in the programming of our culture and its hypnotic suggestions about who we are and how to become deserving of these life-nutrients that provide personhood and community. At some point in life we all experience this sense of dislocation regardless of our differences. Some have even suggested that we carry the wounds and traumas of our ancestors. Others suggest that this sense of disconnection is intrinsic to the quest of being human. Though the prescribed causes may be debatable, the effects of our dislocation are clear.

My Story

She wore a thick white cotton blouse, as did the other girls. Hers was starched and remained that way all day, clean and fitted at the waist with a broad band of fabric. Her bright green skirt was perfectly pleated and it too remained that way through multiple sittings in the hot classroom that was second grade for well near seventy students. But she stood out. She was the teacher's daughter. For me, it was not for that reason that she caught my eye; it was for her seeming perfection. I idolized her. She wore her hair in perfectly parted plaits tied with bobbles that kept their place.

I did not keep mine.

She was copper toned. In Jamaica, today we say she was a "browning." Her mother was equally brown. At that time in Jamaica teaching was the profession of the upper classes. Central Branch Primary School, though a "down town" school, was well respected because of its headmistress and attracted a mixture of students from poor working class families, middle class aspirants and scions of the wealthy.

I was the son of aspirants. And black like coal.

I played hard. I was not the fastest runner, but I ran. Peter Anderson was always first to the wall at the end of the playing field—a race that began at the start of the lunch bell.

In the tussle of the playing field I let it slip that I liked her.

I do not recall how it all happened, and I will not make it up here since that lost detail is immaterial to that overall memory. What I do recall is that somehow our teacher found out that I "liked" her daughter.

I remember clearly standing alone in that classroom as the firestorm from that woman's mouth rained down on me. I had lost my place. I had dared to think and make it known that I liked her daughter. The class laughed and I disappeared from everyone and from myself. I had become worthless in their eyes, so I became invisible to hide my shame.

From then on I was the abandoned and invisible man. In the back of my mind I said to myself: "I'll show them." That was the only tool for survival I had. I would work long, hard, and alone, and though they had underestimated me, in the long run I would emerge and outshine them all.

In school at Calabar High, my classmate, Raymond Goulboure, called me the self-made man—a reference to Thomas Wolsey, Lord Chancellor to Henry VIII. Usually worn as a badge of honor—a defining pride—that decision made in my young awareness shaped much of my identity until the moment I chose to confront my choice.

Until then work was always covering up the shame and loneliness that took root in me that day. Among other things overwork defined a relationship in which all I did was work, spending little quality time with my partner. I was always working at perfecting something and promising something since promises made me valuable and seen. Mostly it was fear of shame that caused me to deliver on them. When I was asked how I was doing I answered by saying how my work was going. For many years into my adult life looking good was more important than being well. Though some would say I have many accomplishments, I struggle to see them myself. People often say that I am charming and creative, but I don't own the compliment because I cannot see it myself. Today, I am learning to see myself with new eyes.

Perhaps no single incident tells the complete story about how we are disconnected from life's nutrients, but this one resonates for me. It marks the place where I was disconnected from my ability to see my own value and feel connected to others. From that point on, value and connection were ideals I had to create outside of myself.

GUIDEPOST 3.
DO THIS NOW

In your journal reflect as deeply as you can on the following questions:

1. *Where in your life would you say that you FIRST experienced wounding—a disconnection from one or more of the LIFE-NUTRIENTS? What happened?*

2. *How did that experience make you feel?*

- ☐ *Silenced / Dumb / Irrelevant*
- ☐ *Hopeless / Lost*
- ☐ *Worthless / Invisible*
- ☐ *Abandoned / Betrayed / Lonely*
- ☐ *Homeless / Unsafe*

3. *What decisions did you make then about life, about who you are and how you would survive?*

WHAT HAPPENS WHEN WE ARE DISCONNECTED

AS WE GROW FROM CHILDHOOD into adulthood we will experience strong emotions that overwhelm and disconnect us from a powerful internal source. In tandem with this disconnection is a culture that tells us that what fulfills us is to be acquired externally and that we must compete with each other for limited resources. This fulfillment is defined as the power we have over others, our ability to control outcomes, what we can buy, who we know, who we can get to like us, and the security of our homes. When we are wounded and then socialized in this way our connection to our own power becomes obscured and we begin to look outside of ourselves to things and to others for some external drug, whatever it may be ("love", sex, money, alcohol, narcotics, food, work, shopping, etc.), craving the memory of the nutrients that give us life.

These are the life-nutrients that fulfill both our needs and desires to be listened to, be hopeful, acknowledged, connected, and part of a safe community.

Think of any action you have ever taken and you will find one or more of these desires at its core. They are the motivation behind every complaint, every expression of gratitude, and every act of war.

As we are disappointed by our misdirected external craving for these life-nutrients our internal connection to them is slowly forgotten. The violence of disconnection leaves wounds. These wounds are protected by attendant fears—feelings of irrelevance, loneliness, hopelessness, shame, and vulnerability—that are triggered in our relationships with family, co-workers, and friends.

This dilemma/cycle of fear and craving—looking outside of ourselves for life's nutrients, while fearing the pain of being hurt again—keeps us stuck at the crossroads of our lives and manifests in the ways described below.

Lying

We Don't Keep Our Word

THE FIRST SIGN that we are out of balance or disconnected from life's nutrients is our inability to give or keep our word to others and to ourselves. Instead we waffle between over-promising or promising nothing at all. In so doing we misrepresent who we are, and what we can do. When our speaking is not congruent with our actions, or misrepresents the facts of our lives, this is clear evidence of our misalignment.

Generally, this imbalance signals a disconnection from the life-nutrient VOICE. It is our voice that channels who we are, where we are, and helps us negotiate our way in the world. It connects us to the present moment. It expresses who, when, where, how, and why—coordinates that help us locate each other in time and space.

When we cannot voice our position, keep our promises, and adjust and communicate them as necessary, we feel that we are not in control of life's circumstances, that we cannot see ourselves and our way clearly, that we do not know the impact of our words on others who rely on them, and the world appears as a chaotic place.

Reconnecting and realigning with all the life-nutrients begins with restoring our connection to the life-nutrient of VOICE.

Masking

We put on 'masks' that turn our best qualities into shadows of themselves

What is a mask you may ask? A behavioral mask is perfectly matched to shield us emotionally from the type of wound we have experienced and helps us to get a temporary hit of the nutrient with which we've lost connection.

These masks emerge from the shadows of our best qualities. For example, it is a wound that causes someone who is naturally organized to become a "control freak" when she confronts the thought—the memory of the pain—that she will be abandoned and left all alone to pull things off by herself. Disconnection can cause people who are naturally charming and eloquent to become insufferable divas, "show-offs" or "dazzlers," always making big promises on which they seldom deliver when they fear invisibility, loss of value, or irrelevance. This also happens when natural nurturers become "martyrs" to the needs of others in order to feel valued and to belong.

Eventually we identify ourselves as these masks that hide our true brilliance and genius and negatively impact our abilities to deliver our gifts.

Our masks are embodiments of our "shadows."

Carl G. Jung said this about the shadow:

> *"The SHADOW describes the part of the psyche that an individual would rather not acknowledge. It contains the denied parts of the self...Bringing shadow material into consciousness drains its dark power, and can even recover valuable resources from it. The greatest power, however, comes from having accepted your shadow parts and integrated them as components of your Self. Everyone carries a SHADOW, and the less it is embodied in the individual's conscious life, the blacker and denser it is. At all counts it forms an unconscious snag, thwarting our most well-meant intentions. One does not become enlightened by imagining figures of light, but by making the darkness conscious."*

It is our shadows and their masks that keep us out of balance.

Competing

We become either victims or victors

WHEN WE LOSE SIGHT of our internal connection to these life-nutrients we will seek them externally by gaining power over things and people. In order to gain power, we will either cast ourselves as victims or victors.

As victims, we will spend much of our time complaining about people and situations that will not do what we want them to in order to make us feel good—heard, hopeful, seen, appreciated, loved, and safe. Casting ourselves as the victim can be very satisfying in as much as it allows us to be rescued by external forces, thus justifying the worldview that power is always external.

If we are not taking the victim route to power and control, we will take the route of getting the nutrients we need at the expense of others. As tyrants, we will use the same complaints that victims use to justify hogging the limelight while not acknowledging others, seeking company but not being a true friend, demanding to be heard while not listening, moving forward yet holding others back, and procuring material wealth and a safe haven while denying others the same.

Addiction

We develop chemical dependencies

MOST SIGNIFICANTLY IF WE FEEL DEPRIVED of these life-nutrients we may try to create a sense of vitality by looking for these nutrients externally from substances. Some of us will use drugs, sex, or food to manipulate our body chemistry to create highs, which eventually become lows. However, the means of high creation that is most commonly used is <u>thinking</u>. We do this by dwelling on our past or an imagined future—projecting hoped for pleasures, or experiences we wish to avoid. These scenarios release powerful internal chemicals to which we become addicted because those chemicals give us a sense of being alive as either victors or victims.

When we live in the past we remember the places where we were deprived of voice, hope, and visibility, where we were rejected and felt chaotic. We remember and are regretful. We spend our time plotting how not to have that happen to us again, how to repeat the ways in which we got our highs in the past, or dreaming about how those highs may come in the future.

This repeated cycle keeps us in our comfort zone where what's important is not what we are focused on. What seems most important is obtaining the drug that past or future based thinking creates to relieve the discomfort of feeling too bad or feeling too good when our identities are not big and spacious enough to hold either.

When we become slaves to our feelings, all of our energy is devoted to the struggle to feel better. Feeling tired, stressed, and depressed our immune system shuts down because the energy it needs is being used in the struggle. In so doing we begin to atrophy and open ourselves to disease.

Obsessing

We overdo activities
in the five areas of life

WHEN WE ARE DISCONNECTED, we overdo activities in the five areas of our lives. We do this at work, at play, and even in our caring for others. We do this even though we say we would rather not. We do this in ways that jeopardize our own well-being.

For example, though being visible and valued is an essential life-nutrient, in the life-area of work, our goals, accomplishments, and financial rewards will not give us a sustained experience of value (self-worth) without the inner eyes to see and value ourselves. Similarly, the activities of having fun and thrill-seeking cannot give us a sustained sense of hope and possibility without us also knowing the soulful inner adventure of our being. Having all the friends or lovers in the world will not give us the experience of an authentic connection with others without us also deeply embracing all of our selves. All our good deeds, sacrifices, and struggles for our communities will not yield a lasting sense of safety and belonging without us first being at home with our selves.

Without an inner connection to life's nutrients, externalized actions become addictive for the temporary high they deliver. When we overdo activities in any one life-area, we disengage with other vital life-areas and the nutrients those areas provide.

In the chapter about the five life-areas we will continue to look more closely at what these areas are and the reasons and ways in which we become obsessed within each area and dependent on the life-nutrients each provides.

THE FIVE COMPLAINTS OF THE EGO

WHEN WE HAVE LOST TOUCH with our connection to life's nutrients in addition to the behaviors of lying, masking, competing, addiction and obsessing, we also become an assemblage of five basic thought patterns that are voiced as complaints. These complaints are the meanings we give to things, based on our experiences of disconnection.

I call them the **Five Complaints of the Ego**. These are the so-called "voices in our head"—the things we say over and over to ourselves, giving voice to them repeatedly. They are the thoughts of the untransformed ego as it struggles to survive change. The hallmark of the Five Complaints of the Ego is that they are repeated consistently with a tone of finality. Distinct from insightful realizations that cause us to take action or call for help, the Five Complaints of the Ego become the thematic tone to which we live our lives.

Each theme below represents one of the five basic voices in our head. When you can identify a theme, you can also identify the life-nutrient from which you are disconnected.

Here they are:

MINERAL	THE STRATEGIST: *"I am lost and confused. I wonder why and what if. I can't figure it out. I don't know how."* This is the voice of one that feels confused and cannot find the logic and purpose of things. These statements indicate that the life-nutrient VOICE—the ability to hear oneself—is depleted.
NATURE	THE DOOMSAYER: *"I am stuck. Things are not moving fast enough. This should not be the way it is."* This is the voice of one that cannot feel the inner movement and vitality of things. This indicates a disconnection from the life-nutrient HOPE—the ability to be in the presence of life as it is.
FIRE	THE FIXER: *"People [myself included] and the things around me are broken and need fixing."* This is the voice that cannot see wholeness beneath the surface of things. It indicates a loss of the life-nutrient VISIBILITY.
WATER	THE JUDGE: *"I am right, they are wrong."* This is the voice that feels disconnected and separate from others. Said often enough it indicates a loss of the life-nutrient CONNECTION.
EARTH	THE PROTECTOR: *"People are doing things to me to make me feel like I don't belong—life is not safe."* This is the voice of one that feels displaced and unsafe. This voice indicates a loss of connection to the life-nutrient BELONGING.

These voices reflect the meaning we make of our human experience when our connection to life's source of nourishment is broken. These are the things we say about ourselves and say about others that block the delivery of our gifts.

IN SUMMARY, WITHOUT AN INNER CONNECTION to life's nutrients, we cannot confront the dissonance created by our externalized cravings for power, our wounds and their attendant fears. In this energetic vacuum, we are held hostage by addictive behaviors, unsatisfying work, dysfunctional relationships, and poor self-care. These are the actions that keep us moving in circles, repeating the same patterns and habits, while neglecting our gifts.

In the following chapter I will share three practices to help us powerfully re-establish and maintain our internal connection to each of the five life-nutrients, break the paralyzing cycle and return to balance, health and growth!

In upcoming chapters I will continue using the elements as metaphors to show us how to:

1. **Identify and better balance activities in the five life-areas.**
   We will learn to use each of the five life-areas as ritual spaces in which to refresh our connection and expand our experience of ourselves in unprecedented ways, rather than relying on our work, family, leisure, and community lives and activities to give us the experiences of visibility, hope, connection, and safety that are best sourced internally.

2. **Find our own unique path of personal "becoming."** This

path of inner balance lies between the shadows of our best qualities and the new qualities we have wanted to experience. We will discover our best qualities and the shadowy masks we wear when negotiating between our fears and our desires.

3. **Slay our fears.** We will identify the wounds and attendant fears to which we are vulnerable and learn how to design powerful personal rituals to help integrate these fears into our best selves.

GUIDEPOST 4.
DO THIS NOW

In your journal reflect on the following:

1. Where in your life can you see that you are not being truthful with others or yourself by:

א *Keeping silent or not speaking your truth*

א *Not keeping your word and failing to adjust your promises as circumstances unfold*

א *Understating or overstating your truth about your value*

א *Having unrealistic expectations of others*

א *Hiding from the facts or the figures*

2. Review the three things you wrote at the end of Chapter 1 that you want to accomplish during this journey, but experience being stopped or delayed in their achievement.

א *Which of the Five Complaints of the Ego have you been saying to yourself about what is stopping or delaying you? You may not be saying them in the exactly the same way, but how are you saying them to yourself? Write them down in your journal.*

א *Imagine if you did not have these complaints around your goals, what might you be able to hear, experience, see, connect to, and produce? Specifically, what new ideas might you hear that you have not allowed yourself to hear before? What new ways of looking at things might emerge? What conversations could you now have and what requests might you now make? Who could you now connect with and how? What could you make?*

Begin to imagine what living in this world might look and feel like. Write this down in your journal.

Keep checking in with yourself as you move towards your goals. The Five Complaints of the Ego is a simple lens through which you can observe your thinking and the way it casts your world, influences your speaking, and determines what you are able to accomplish.

CHAPTER IV

REMEMBERING OUR CONNECTION TO LIFE'S NUTRIENTS

THE NEED TO RESTORE OUR CONNECTION to all of life's nutrients is what we are calling in our current culture the need for "life balance." Yet we live in a modern culture in which we have been socialized to believe that these nutrients—VOICE, HOPE, VISIBILITY, CONNECTION, and BELONGING—exist outside of ourselves and are in short supply.

For instance, advertisers know just how badly we are searching for these essentials. This is why we are sold so many gadgets with powerful technologies that promise to give us the connections we lack. Social media appears to ensure that we are heard, seen, connected, and have a sense of belonging. Virtual games fill our need for change and movement, giving us a sense of danger, risk, and play. Fashion brands aim to help us craft our personal style—giving us a voice.

When our search for these life-nutrients is only external and the need for visibility is overemphasized, our feeling of connection—our ability to relate to and feel for others—is often diminished. When the need for connection is overdone, our unique voice and self-care can be compromised. When the need for belonging is over-done, our ability to have HOPE—to dream, to play, and to go on adventures— is diminished. However, these life-nutrients work in tandem with each other when activated from a single internal source.

Imagine that we travel across the landscape of our lives trying to get the five vital life-nutrients we need, believing that they are in short supply, assuming that someone or something will give them to us if we do the right thing. Tragically, when we are distracted from our internal nutrient source we lose vital pieces of the psychological bridge that allows us to grow naturally and deliver our gifts to the world.

How do we begin to restore our connection?

Here is a practice designed to revitalize that connection.

THE FIVE DECLARATIONS OF THE SELF

To begin to restore a conscious connection with life's nutrients, we must start with the idea that we have these nutrients and abilities intact within ourselves and that there is a place within us where this connection is unbroken. There are five declarations that when said with feeling can help to powerfully refresh our connec-

tion. Each declaration is a simple yet powerful state-
ment.

These declarations counter the Five Complaints of the Ego.

They are five elementally calibrated declarations that when con-
templated and spoken sequentially will activate all five nutrient
sources, reawakening our memory of our own voices, the experience
of growth, our vision of ourselves in the world, the experience of connection to all others, and our sense of safety and belonging in the
world.

Here they are.

MINERAL

I can Hear Myself

NATURE

I Can Feel Myself Changing

FIRE

I Can See Myself

WATER

I Am Connected to All Life

EARTH

I Am Home.

Practicing the Declarations

SOME AWKWARDNESS CAN accompany the initial practice of these declarations. The declarations will be confusing for the ego—the part of us that requires proof and operates based on the basic five physical senses and a settled identity. There may be feelings of disorientation as the ego tries to look for evidence of the truth in what's being said in ways that are familiar to it. Stay with the practice. Don't stop.

With these declarations, we are beginning to help the ego remember and express its connection to the source. The disorientation is necessary for a new soulful identity based on an expanded awareness to emerge.

GUIDEPOST 5.
BEGIN THIS PRACTICE NOW

At the start of each new day become still. Close your eyes. Ground yourself with a feeling of gratitude and acceptance. **This means you are not trying to change anything. Dismiss any concept that arises of how your present situation should be. Do not visualize or imagine anything.**
Pause after each line, take a deep, slow breath and listen to the spaces of silence between each statement.

After you have said all five lines sit still for a while with your eyes closed and observe the sensations in your body—make room in your awareness for the physical sensations, thoughts, and emotions that arise.

Keep deepening your connection by doing as many cycles of the five affirmations with breathing, stillness, and observation as your time allows. Notice if the space between each cycle begins to expand. If it does, spend more time there.

Remember *to* practice these declarations without ANY visualization. The words in the declarations above are the essence of the declarations. As we first start our practice reciting them is all that is necessary. We don't need to know how to experience a declaration. When we say each declaration, we may experience a gap between what we are saying and our idea of what images the declaration should conjure. This is good. Through that gap an adjustment is being made. Be present with any physical sensation or discomfort within the gap.

As we deepen this practice we can extend each declaration to apply to any situation we are currently experiencing. Here are some examples from my own practice.

- *I can hear myself. Next steps and ideas are coming to mind, in pictures seen, words read, dreams, and coincidences. I can hear the story of my life and its purpose being read— the story about who I am and what I am becoming.*
- *I can feel myself changing. Despite discomfort and appearances life is changing now to reveal more of who I really am—my desire for greater joy, order, and balance. I can feel everything changing now.*
- *I can see myself. Through light and in shadow, fear and desire, in the simplicity of things, just the way they are now, I can see myself with pure eyes, my goodness, essence, excellence, and possibility.*
- *I am connected to life. I can feel this regardless of challenging emotions, differing opinions, and points of view. Despite our different points of view, I can feel my connection to all others and to all of nature.*
- *I am home. I am safe in the world. There is no need to rush*

anything. Everything is timely and in order. I cannot be moved. I am at rest. I am home.

When we notice the Five Complaints of the Ego we must simply accept them, recognize their source, and counter them with the matching five declarations. Again, this is not just an exercise in positive thinking.

With this practice of noticing and declaring we are prompting the ego to remember and express its connection to Source.

Five Complaints	Five Declarations
"I wonder why and what if?"	I can Hear Myself
"I am stuck. This should not be..."	I Can Feel Myself Changing.
"Fix me. Fix you. Fix it."	I Can See Myself
"I am right; they are wrong"	I Am Connected to ALL Life
"Life is not safe..."	I Am Home.

Remember these declarations because they will be put to further use in ritual spaces in the final chapter of this book. In that chapter nature based rituals will be introduced as yet another way to strengthen and celebrate our connection with life's nutrient source.

Finally, as we deepen our practice, these declarations will eventually begin to enter our conscious thought as we go about our day. Soon they will influence our speaking and be reflected in our actions towards ourselves and others.

Honoring Your Connection

Practice bringing honor to your connection to life's nutrient source by looking for and appreciating the simplest moments in which you display the abilities these nutrients provide. Acknowledgement is a practice to help us increase our awareness of the things that really matter.

Acknowledging Yourself

GUIDEPOST 6.
BEGIN THIS PRACTICE NOW
At the end of each day review your day and acknowledge yourself for the times:

1. *When you spoke truthfully in your own voice or made space to hold someone else's truth.*
2. *When you stepped beyond a limiting thought and barrier or inspired another to do the same.*
3. *When you saw your own value and the difference your presence made, or when you saw and acknowledged that in another.*
4. *When you acted on your connection and felt compassion for another or when someone reached out to you in this manner.*
5. *When, though you were vulnerable, you felt safe and protected or made someone feel that way.*

Each time we acknowledge ourselves in these ways we strengthen our connection with the life-giving nutrients—the things we all need to BLOOM.

Acknowledging Others

Acknowledging someone is one of the most powerful gifts that we can bestow. When we give it freely to each other it has the power to liberate us. An acknowledgment finds the best point of view on the events of our lives. It shows that we recognize the good in spite of appearances. It lets us know that we truly see and are truly seen. By acknowledging one another we demonstrate that we know that together we can have and hold it all. Through acknowledgement we feel our shared joys and pains, and give ourselves unlimited room to grow.

GUIDEPOST 7.
BEGIN THIS PRACTICE NOW
Begin to notice the people in your life and verbally acknowledge them for:

1. *Listening to your truth and for speaking and living their truth.*
2. *Stepping beyond a limiting thought and barrier and inspiring you to do the same.*
3. *Adding value to your life and making a difference for you by being who they are.*

4. *Reaching out and connecting across differences and misun-
   derstandings.*

5. *Creating a safe space for you to be completely at home.*

Each day, find someone to acknowledge. Make it a practice.

With these simple practices, we are beginning to take the first steps towards exploring the inner terrain of life balance. There will be deeper inner work to do in the upcoming chapters, but first let's explore the five life-areas in which we all have activities. Let's take a look at how and why we overdo activities in each area, and how to better use each area to express and strengthen our inner sense of balance.

CHAPTER V

THE FIVE LIFE-AREAS

I N THE LAST CHAPTER, we were introduced to the five life-nutrients that support our growth. There, the five elements of
mineral, nature, fire, water, and earth were used as metaphors
to help us understand the things we need to feel balanced and to
grow. As explained in the previous chapter these nutrients *must first
be sourced from within* and expressed as a growing sense of accomplishment and feeling of balance. Here are these nutrients:

1. MINERAL which gives us VOICE—the ability to hear
    and express ourselves uniquely.
2. NATURE which gives us the ability to HOPE—to experi-
    ence ourselves and our circumstances as growing and
    changing for the better.
3. FIRE which gives us VISIBILITY—allowing us to truly
    see and value ourselves and others.
4. WATER which gives us a sense of CONNECTION—al-

lowing us to feel related to others and connected to a common source.

5. EARTH which gives us an experience of BELONG-ING—allowing us to experience a sense of home and stability.

The last chapter looked at what happens when we are disconnected from our nutrient source and contained a practice to help us renew our internal connection with these vital life-nutrients.

In this chapter, we will take a look at the five life-areas we engage each day of our lives to experience and express these life-nutrients. These are the "five life-areas" in which all human beings have activities. Again, we will use the five elements as metaphors to help us see and better understand each of the five life-areas.

Activities are simply the actions we perform in each life-area. An activity can be a long-term PROJECT or a one-time TASK. Included also are PRACTICES—things that we do on a regular basis to create specific results (for example, saving money to reach a specific goal) or to have a desired experience (for example, getting eight hours of sleep to feel more rested).

These five life-areas are a pretty comprehensive map of all human endeavors and work in an inter-connected way to support our journey to find a new center of balance.

Here are the five life-areas and their elemental associations:

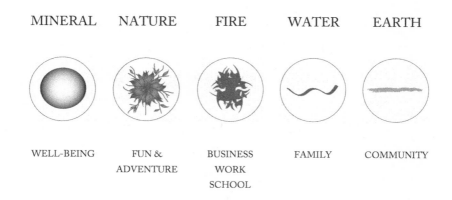

MINERAL   NATURE   FIRE   WATER   EARTH

WELL-BEING   FUN &   BUSINESS   FAMILY   COMMUNITY
             ADVENTURE   WORK
                          SCHOOL

Each life-area is a ritual place or playground to experience and express the vital life-nutrients of VOICE, HOPE, VISIBILITY, CONNECTION, and BELONGING. Here are the life-areas, each with their element and life-nutrient association.

MINERAL   NATURE   FIRE   WATER   EARTH

WELL-BEING   FUN &   BUSINESS   FAMILY   COMMUNITY
             ADVENTURE   WORK
                          SCHOOL

VOICE   HOPE   VISIBILITY   CONNECTION   SAFETY
             CHANGE   VALUE   BELONGING

1. WELL-BEING [Mineral] is the life-area in which we per-
    form activities to nurture and express our unique VOICE
    though self-care.

2. FUN & ADVENTURE [Nature] is the life-area in which we experience CHANGE and demonstrate our ability to be HOPEFUL through play and leisure time alone or with others.

3. BUSINESS / JOB / SCHOOL [Fire] is the life-area in which we express how we SEE ourselves and our VALUE through work or study.

4. FAMILY [Water] is the life-area in which we honor our CONNECTION to all life by creating families of blood and choice.

5. COMMUNITY [Earth] is the life-area in which we create and experience SAFETY and BELONGING by creating a home and community for ourselves and others.

Life-Areas as Ritual Spaces

Each life-area is a personal ritual space—a place to practice and cultivate our personal growth. Each area of life—community, family, work, play, and health—is meant to be approached with awareness and intention. Each life-area is a place of discovery, where we go to "find" - or better said, "remember" ourselves. Activities in each life-area are acts best intended to reveal and express deepening levels of self-awareness as we grow.

However, if we approach activities in a life-area without first being clear that activity's life-nutrient is sourced internally, we will overdo activities in that area. Such externalized activities will become addictive behaviors, designed to avoid feelings of irrelevance, hopelessness, worthlessness, loneliness, or homelessness. This over-burden and addiction is happening in many of our lives and much of our culture.

Each life-area is meant to be a space in which to strengthen our inner experience of specific life-nutrients to help us remember and reveal what is already present in us.

THE NEW LIFE-CYCLE

THINK OF THESE FIVE LIFE-AREAS as a new kind of "bicycle" that doesn't just have two wheels called "work" and "life," but rather five wheels upon which we must learn to balance. We can think of them as our new "life-cycle." Before we start riding, though, let us take a moment to look at the parts and connections and how they work. Let's take a look at each wheel—its rim, spokes, and tire—and visualize how to get the entire apparatus started.

Just like a bicycle, riding well can give us an incredible experience of balance and motion, and take us to previously inaccessible places. Mastering this new apparatus can open unexplored inner experiences and new external worlds. How we choose to use the mechanism will determine what we can accomplish in life—how deeply we will go to find and celebrate ourselves.

Let's now take a closer look at each of the life-areas. Bear in mind that these life-areas often overlap each other creating hybrid areas of activity such as those in the area of BUSINESS: the family-business, leisure-business, social-entrepreneurship, not-for-profits, hospitals, etc.

Knowledge of each life-area in its purest form will help us understand how to negotiate life's terrain—to notice overlapping life-areas, to choose which are dominant and which are stylistic, to see how they are connected and help us better choose how to balance them all. We will then begin to understand where to focus our attention and what new ground to take and when.

Life-Area #1
MINERAL

WELL-BEING

The first life-area of "WELL-BEING." It is home to activities meant to nurture and celebrate our personal, spiritual, social, mental, emotional, and physical well-being. Again, it is the life-area associated with MINERAL since these activities of self-care empower our unique VOICE and self-expression, allowing us to experience the unique narrative about who we are, and empowering us to speak that narrative clearly in the world.

Think of this area as "first gear." It is the place to start. If you find that you must stop and regain your sense of balance in life, come back to this area to begin again. On your list of daily things-to-do make the well-being life-area your first priority.

Our spiritual well-being includes activities we perform as individuals to connect to our idea of GOD or a source that is invisible. These are practices observed on our own that can involve our ideas of prayer or meditation. Our social well-being is supported by activities during which we move freely among and observe other human beings who are changing. Our mental well-being is supported by activities that keep our minds sharp, inspire insight, and reveal new challenging perspectives. In this life-area we also take care of our physical and emotional health with diet and exercise and doing what it takes to experience and accept our feelings.

Life-Area #2
NATURE

FUN & ADVENTURE

This is the area we visit to consciously cultivate and experience change. This is the area in which we risk our identities. It is where we play and have adventures with others, where we converse with others, where we explore nature and have sexual intercourse. It is where we take risks and explore boundaries. It is where we go on vacation, have leisure time and travel to new places alone or with people we love. This is where we meet others and decide how we will interact with them—determining whether or not we want to support each other, create more adventures together, develop working relationships, build a family, or pursue a cause together.

The intention in this area is to perform these activities for no other reason than to honor our sense of being alive in the moment. These are activities or practices that enlarge us by taking us out of our comfort zones. These include fun things that we will do by ourselves or with others. They may be nature-based activities that put us in touch with "growing things."

Activities in this life-area are rituals for personal change and transformation. People who make time for FUN & PLAY develop a great capacity for navigating sudden change and have a greater sense of HOPE.

Many of our most innovative ideas don't really start in the life-area of BUSINESS (which we will talk about in a minute). Some of the best ideas come from the first two life-areas—Well-Being and Fun & Adventure. They come when we are relaxed, when we are well, when we are exercising, being still, when we are outdoors in nature, hanging with friends and "shooting the breeze." We then take those ideas to the business domain to create them and make them visible, or we take them to our families to build stronger connections, or into our communities to help us cause something to happen together.

Life-Area #3
FIRE

BUSINESS/WORK
SCHOOL

This life-area is a composite of the three ways in which we pursue and express our lives' passions through our jobs, businesses, or school. It is where our value is seen and honored by others. In this area, you learn about and create products and services in exchange for value. After FUN & ADVENTURE this is the area in which we answer the question, "What can we create together to expresses our gifts and talents?"

This is where we identify and pursue goals that best express our gifts by creating a business, finding a job, or taking a course of study. Through these activities, we have opportunities to be seen and valued as the individuals we really are.

This life-area supports our need for VISIBILITY. People who are actualized in this area have a great sense of accomplishment and VALUE. When activities in this life-area are overdone or underdone, issues involving the fear of rejection, shame, or being perceived as worthless may be indicated. Additionally, because of the cultural framing of this life-area as the central counterweight to all the others on the two-sided scale called "work-life balance" many people spend most of their time and effort here.

Life-Area #4
WATER

FAMILY

This is the life-area in which we connect with and care for others. FAMILY here is not limited to our blood families. These are the people with whom we are going to create something; whether it is a home, an experience, or children. Often people in business or working in community become a family and start to care deeply about each other. FAMILY is the space we create to honor ancestry and nourish and maintain relationships. This area includes activities that entail coupling, creating a home, parenting, and taking care of elders and relatives. These activities are rituals that honor the continuity and inter-relatedness of life.

Life-Area #5
EARTH

COMMUNITY

This life-area primarily supports our need for safety. Activities in the area of COMMUNITY provide opportunities for us to experience the stability and belonging we crave. It is a place of power where things are nurtured, where people get together to cause something to happen for the good of the planet and all humanity. This is where we have fellowship, where we volunteer, and where we plot political and social action. This is where gifts are given and received, where organizations are joined and where the environment is protected and maintained for a new generation. The power to cause something communally affects how safe we feel on the planet.

The activities in this life-area engage us in genuine giving without thought of the benefits to ourselves. These activities may include philanthropic, political, or environmental action. These are activities that ground us and strengthen our sense of safety and place in the world.

Here is an expanded version of the five primary life-areas and the five secondary areas of each.

THE LIFE AREA CHART

MINERAL	NATURE	FIRE	WATER	EARTH
WELL-BEING	**FUN & ADVENTURE**	**BUSINESS/ WORK**	**FAMILY**	**COMMUNITY**
Spiritual	Alone Time	Planning & Visioning	Birthing, Dying & Ancestry	Fellowship
Social	Sense Pleasure	Information & Communication Systems	Family Traditions & Rituals	Political & Social Action
Mental	Risk & Competition	Financial Management	Personal & Family Financials	Philanthropy & Economic Development
Emotional	Group Play & Adventure	Team Building & Facilitation	Quality Time	Organizational Memberships
Physical	Nature Activities	Production	Homemaking	Environment

How to Use Each Area As a Ritual Space

The FIVE LIFE-AREAS are not a prescription for life balance. They are simply a set of lenses, or a mirror by which we can notice our imbalance and make the appropriate adjustments. Remember, balance is not a fixed place or formula; it is a fluid inner experience from which all things bloom!

Each LIFE-AREA is a ritual space where activities are performed with the intention to deepen connection to and expression of the five life-nutrients.

- ℵ We go to WELL-BEING to engage in practices that celebrate, honor, and amplify our unique VOICE and self-expression—who we <u>already</u> are and what gifts we possess. There we mediate, we forgive, we inspire, we feel, and we move.

- ℵ We go to FUN & ADVENTURE not just as pleasure seekers, but in celebration and expression of our ability to experience CHANGE and growth. Here we dialog, have sex, play outdoors, sit quietly, or jump from planes.

- ℵ We engage in BUSINESS to honor, celebrate, and contribute our VALUE to the world and to make VISIBLE what we see and know of ourselves. We plan, communicate, work with others, and generate products and services that reflect our beauty.

- ℵ We engage with FAMILY to deepen our CONNEC-

TION with all life by honoring our mothers, fathers, sisters, and brothers even if they are not blood relatives and whether they are unknown, deceased, or miserable.

א We go to COMMUNITY spaces to celebrate our inner sense of being at HOME and sense of BELONGING. This is where we engage in fellowship, mentor, give, organize politically and take care of the Earth.

Our activities in each life-area should be a reminder and celebration of the inner connection we have with each of the five life-nutrients. If the life-areas are not engaged as ritual creative spaces - as places of remembering - then the areas lose their power and become traps in which we try to get from the external environment and from others in that life-area, nutrients they cannot give us.

Life-nutrients must first be sourced internally. Ultimately, externalized activity and internal connection with these nutrients must work in tandem if we are to experience a sense of balance. For example, being in business without knowing your value can lead to undercharging for goods and services, yet it is the activity of business that is intended to remind us of our value. Being in business, seeking primarily a sense of connection and relationship, subverts the energy of the area and diminishes its power as a place where value is seen, given, and rewarded.

When we come to these spaces with our brokenness we must approach them as healing spaces, with the awareness of their power to rekindle and help us remember and celebrate our inner connection to the life-nutrient housed in each life-area.

How Madra Spends Her Time

Here is what Madra noticed about how she spent her time after learning about the five life-areas.

WELL-BEING—10 percent of her time

FUN & ADVENTURE—15 percent. She spent a lot of time hanging out with her friends and talking about her ideas, imagining, and fantasizing about her life.

WORK—65 percent. She spent most of her day working, but not really at the things she said she wanted. How did she spend her time?   Much of her time was spent in her head, fighting with her fears and debating with people who wanted to help her with her project. It was spent trying to arrange meetings and correcting things she'd said because she was seldom clear with others about what she wanted.

FAMILY—10%. Her family was neglected. She went up the Bronx "once in a blue moon" to see her mom. Her romantic relationship dried up because her partner felt she was always working.

COMMUNITY—0%. Although she had an intention to give back, at the end of the day she had nothing left to give to anyone else.

BY NOW YOU MAY be beginning to reflect on your own lives and noticing where you are spending our time and making judgments about this. It is good that we are noticing these things, but slow down, remember we are just beginning to see the basics of the new life balancing apparatus.

In the next chapter, we will take a deeper look at the inner-skills that will help us develop our own unique styles of negotiating these life-areas and reconnecting to life balancing nutrients and expressing them. We will look at some specific ways in which each of us as individuals can use this new apparatus since each of us expresses balance in unique ways. How we will use our new "life cycle" to carve out our unique styles, paths and centers of gravity is up to us. We will take a look at the three unique key personality traits we each possess as well as their accompanying shadows that throw us off balance. We will learn how to keep moving forward.

But first take this quiz.

GUIDEPOST 8.
DO THIS NOW

Note: The following questions are intended to help you become more aware of how you are spending your time and the motivation behind your choices. After you answer all the questions, re-read the chapter, reflect on your responses, and journal about your insights.

1. *In your journal quickly write down all five life-areas outlined in this chapter and without thinking too deeply write down beside each one the percentage of time you spend in each.*

      _____ % WELL-BEING

_____ % FUN & ADVENTURE

_____ % BUSINESS / WORK / SCHOOL

_____ % FAMILY

_____ % COMMUNITY

2. What LIFE-NUTRIENTS are you most hoping to find in the area where you spend most of your time?

- ☐ Voice / Relevance
- ☐ Hope / Change / Adventure
- ☐ Visibility / Value / Worth
- ☐ Connection / Relationship
- ☐ Belonging / Safety / Stability

3. As you search for these LIFE-NUTRIENTS, what if anything are you most trying to <u>avoid</u> feeling?

- ☐ Unheard | Irrelevant
- ☐ Stuck | Stagnant | Hopeless
- ☐ Invisible | Worthless | Ashamed
- ☐ Abandoned | Lonely
- ☐ Vulnerable | Chaotic | Defenseless

4. Where are you spending the <u>least</u> amount of time? What life-nutrient might activating that LIFE-AREA provide for you?

- ☐ *Voice*
- ☐ *Hope / Change / Adventure*
- ☐ *Value / Visibility / Worth*
- ☐ *Connection / Relationship*
- ☐ *Belonging / Safety / Stability*

GUIDEPOST 9.
BEGIN THIS PRACTICE NOW

Begin to designate a life-area to each activity as you place it in your calendar. Color-code each event using the colors listed below. This will give you an easy visual way to see how you are spending your time. Doing this will help you to make the adjustments to create a mix of activities that support your sense of balance.

Purple – WELL-BEING
Green – FUN, LEISRE, & ADVENTURE
RED – BUSINESS, WORK, STUDY
BLUE – FAMILY & CLOSE FRIENDS
YELLOW – COMMUNITY

OVER-LAPPING AREAS

IDENTIFYING THE DOMINANT LIFE-AREA for each activity in which you engage (especially activities that seem to land in two or more areas) can be challenging. However, doing so is important, as it will help you find the new center of balance you seek. For instance, some ventures are family-businesses – a mix of the life-areas of FAMILY and BUSNESS; social enterprises are a mix of the life-areas of COMMUNITY and BUSINESS; spiritual communities are mix of the life-areas WELL-BEING and COMMUNITY, and often BUSINESS amongst others.

In these cases, begin to notice the life-area with which you most naturally identify this activity. It has been my observation that one area is usually the more natural designator of the activity and the other life-areas simply indicate the style, values or products and services of the dominant area.

In some family owned businesses – businesses that involve family members or close friends - the life-area BUSINESS is dominant and informs the structure of the business and the main motivation of the enterprise which is profit making. Here, "family" designates the style in which such a business may be conducted and the values to be honored in meeting business objectives. Additionally, if the business produces a healthcare product for example, it also operates in the life-area of WELL-BEING. Here there are multiple areas of activities.

In other such family businesses, FAMILY is the dominant field of activity and the primary basis on which decisions are made. Here the idea of profitability, roles, and functions serve the need of preserving peace and continuity among family and close friends.

The same principles can be applied by those of us running social enterprises, where we often grapple with the need for profitability versus making a difference socially. Creative entrepreneurs and artists may also confront these choices, as well as those of us who make an independent living offering well-being or healing services.

So, again, identifying the dominant life-area of an activity recognizes its fundamental nature, while secondary life-areas indicate the style, products/services, or values; how one goes about doing things.

Again, to be clear, making these distinctions are not simply academic, but will empower us to find the balance we all seek, for two often we get lost in a sea of activities and lose our way.

One could argue that all the life areas are interconnected and that it is possible to satisfy all them in one field of activity. Admittedly a BUSINESS for example, can be about WELL-BEING, FUN & LEISURE, FAMILY, AND COMMUNITY. But FUN & LEISURE time taken with business partners are distinct from the same time taken by yourself for you to honor your own well-being or sense of adventure.

Deciding which life-area an activity fits best is based on what you feel are your real needs are and your motivations for engaging in an activity. The idea here is to do so consciously and intentionally to honor the life-nutrient you need.

NEGOTIATING RELATIONSHIPS IN CHALLENGING AREAS

WE ALL COME TO OUR VARIOUS ROLES in the areas of our lives desiring experiences that are deeply meaningful and fundamental to our survival. We want to be heard, know that things will change for the better, be seen and valued for who we are, connect emotionally with others, and feel that we belong. These needs and desires are the nutrients of life. Knowing which ones we must experience, where, and in what order is subjective, variable and important since we all have differing needs and each area of life provides for different essentials. The relationships we establish within each area of our lives should be negotiated with these needs and desires in mind.

These life nutrients are the drivers behind our assumptions about how others should treat us. When we don't get these needs met we may feel deeply hurt or ashamed because these nutrients are connected to our fears of irrelevance, hopelessness, worthlessness, abandonment and instability. They inform how we move through life, helping us decide which situations to avoid, and where and to whom to go to get what we need.

This is true whatever our roles—whether as parents, employees, friends or partners. We all come loaded with the need for specific life-nutrients.

Additionally, in these roles and life-areas we also seek to give to others and the spaces we inhabit the same fundamentals we desire for ourselves. The life-nutrients we crave also give rise to our passions and talents, such that, for example, people who crave a sense of home and belonging are often natural caregivers, and folks who need connection are often the best a making them and connecting others.

What we each seek, how we prioritize those life-nutrients and how we go about acquiring them is unique to each of us. This uniqueness is shaped in many instances by the ways we have been wounded, the way we now see the world, and the possibility and vision we have for our lives. By understanding each other's special path we can understand better how we can all work together to experience and express that which we must.

Knowing which desires drive us in our various roles and life-areas (oftentimes the same need dominates every life-area we inhabit) will help us to communicate our needs to each other and share more effectively what we each have to give. In this way we can discover together where and when are the most appropriate places for exchange. For example, if we come to business seeking primarily connection, this may not be the space for that, but the need for connection can be acknowledged and space made to accommodate it in the ways we manage, facilitate and reward our business associates, partners and ourselves. Everything can be negotiated. The point is to be conscious and aware of our drivers.

For some of us, myself included, connection is the most important life-nutrient. For others it is value. Others need first to experience change and their power to change things. Others come to find meaning—to make narrative sense of their lives. Some simply need a place to belong—a space to take care of others and call home.

With so many needs existing at once, the trade-offs we make, the bargains we strike to get what we need can be both amazing and problematic. For example, trading in our need to be valued for the greater need to belong. The result can be staying on jobs too long, or remaining in relationships where connection has been lost but a home is still provided. These are the trade-offs we make.

This then is how arrive in our roles, our work places, families, communities and teams: wounded and needing to be made whole, to find our own unique healing salve, to harvest the nutrients we lack, and to express them as our gifts and talents. Beneath our odd behaviors are these needs, these desires, wanting and waiting to be fulfilled and expressed.

GUIDEPOST 10.
DO THIS NOW

1.   Identify a life-area or relationship in which you now feel most challenged –feeling out of balance, unfulfilled or somehow incomplete. This could be in a relationship with a friend, associate, family member, co-worker boss, or in a space of activity, at church, in volunteer organization, a social space, self-care, business or home. What would you say you are you seeking to express and experience most in these relationships and spaces?

- ☐ *VOICE: To find and express a unique narrative in the way you make art, write, philosophize and make sense of the world for yourself and others*
- ☐ *CHANGE: To express and experience hope --the birthing of newness and to feel your power to change and to change things,*
- ☐ *VISIBILITY & VALUE: To be seen and valued for who you really are: to be acknowledged for our life's possibility and promise.*
- ☐ *CONNECTION: To experience friendship and genuine relationships with others: to feel that everyone is*

connected despite obvious differences.

☐ *BELONGING: to have a deep sense of home, and stability: to feel that you are in a safe place from which you cannot be moved.*

Reflect carefully, for often what we think we should prioritize in a life area does to reflect our deepest assumptions and expectations.

2. *After choosing the main life-nutrient you need, and ask yourself:*

   א *"How I go after it?*
   א *When I don't get it how does it make me feel?*
   א *When I don't get it what do you do?*
   א *When I do that, what is the cost to myself and to others?*

3. *For each relationship or space that is challenging ask yourself: "What life-nutrient is this person adept at, or which life-nutrient is this space most designed to provide?*

Ultimately the things we seek --these nutrients must first be sourced within for them to be expressed outwardly and or even received in ways that pure, generative and gracious. In the following chapters we will continue our journey within to find that which we all seek.

CHAPTER VI

KEY ESSENCES & DESIRES

I N THE LAST CHAPTER, we observed that when we overdo one life-area, it is easy to neglect others. For example, working hard, but not exploring equally our passions and gifts through play; serving others, but not valuing our own self-care; being free-spirited, but not being creative; pursuing our individual well-being, but without real engagement with our community.

We overdo activities in choice areas of our lives because we externalize power. We use external objects, people and goals (even noble ones) to give us the experiences we crave—of relevance, hope, visibility, connection, and belonging. We do so often without any real sense of lasting fulfillment.

In truth, we are hindered from finding inner balance and delivering our gifts in ways that are healing for us by the gap between what we crave when we overdo activities and the feelings we must confront should we choose to act differently—feelings of irrelevance, hopelessness, invisibility, loneliness, and homelessness. Together our cravings and our fears keep us stuck in a "no man's land" of sameness where we overdo the same activities and patterns of behavior without any real sense of fulfillment or experience of expansion.

This is a dynamic that we must transform—the storm we must walk through. This means that we will be called upon to allow a new us to emerge, one that can contain the dissonance between our desires and our fears and still move us forward.

In this chapter, we will begin the process of helping ourselves to discover our unique pathways between our specific fears and our desires.

This path is the path of "BECOMING."

INTRODUCING THE ESSENCE CARDS

"WHICH THREE ESSENCE CARDS did you choose that best describe you?" I asked Madra. I was eager to hear her answer. I was referring to the deck of 25 cards I had given her during our first meeting.

A brief word about these cards will provide some context.

These cards describe the 25 distinct human personality archetypes—their light and dark sides. In this deck are the three key qualities that best describe us and our attendant shadows right now. These are called KEY ESSENCES. Also in the deck are the three other desired qualities that balance those KEY ESSENCES. Those qualities are called our DESIRED ESSENCES. When paired together these KEY and DESIRED ESSENCES create a new and dynamic way of understanding our paths to balance and fulfillment.

"I chose six!" she said.

"That's a lot," I replied.

"Why do you say that?" she asked.

"Well... all 25 of the essences are in us, but at different stages of our lives and, depending on what's happening, there are usually three KEY ESSENCES that describe us for better or worse. Tell me about your top three."

"Okay. I chose IMAGINATION," she answered proudly.

"Why and how do you express it?"

"Because I have so many great ideas. People usually love to brainstorm with me and I can show them new ways of looking at things that open up new possibilities for them."

"Did your friends, the people around you, confirm this for you?"

"Yes, they did."

"Okay. So here is how you will know if IMAGINATION is one of your KEY ESSENCES. Ask yourself: What happens when your IMAGINATION goes out of balance or when you overdo it?"

"I couldn't really see myself overdoing it."

"What happens when you are too imaginative?" I probed.

"Well, I spend a lot of time in my head thinking of better ideas and different approaches to avoid certain things. There always seem to be lots of different possibilities."

"I know. It's like spinning around 10,000 versions of the same idea, each more brilliant than the one before. What does this cost you?" I asked.

"Time and the patience of others. It can be a little frustrating for the people I work with. But it's my process."

"What else does it cost you?" I asked gently.

"People don't really take me seriously or think I am going to pull

things off. They always think I am working on the next new idea,"
she laughed nervously.

"But there must be something you get out of doing this since
you keep doing it, right?" I paused. "When you overdo a KEY ES-
SENCE at the cost of something you value there is usually a reason,
something you are after. When you overdo IMAGINATION which
life-nutrient are you trying to experience: VOICE, HOPE, VISI-
BILITY, CONNECTION, or STABILITY?"

"All of the above, I guess. But all the ideas I have are great!" she
insisted.

"I know. And wouldn't having more great ideas make you even
greater?"I added with a chuckle.

"Greatness is a good thing," she said with a laugh in her voice.

"Madra, I want you to consider that when your IMAGINA-
TION goes into overdrive it is being thrown out of balance in order
to provide specific life-nutrients you think you don't have AND to
avoid some fears you do have."

Madra's Key Essences

FOR MADRA, IMAGINATION was the quality that she had a lot
of. She had drawn on it to help her imagine the possibility of life
away from a small town where she'd been unable to be fully herself.
It was the quality that had helped her to imagine her television series.
But it was also the quality that she could not turn off. It took her
down roads where she spent a lot of time imagining the realization
of her dreams and the perils and pitfalls of the same. Among her

friends, she was known as "the dreamer"—the girl with so much potential, but much of it currently unrealized. She always had a good idea for others. She was finding it difficult to establish a clear and consistent direction around which to galvanize the team that volunteered to work with her on her project. IMAGINATION became the way she kept herself HOPEFUL and VISIBLE and helped herself avoid feeling WORTHLESS and STUCK. This had cost her. After five years, her idea, brilliant as it was, was still a dream.

Her second KEY ESSENCE was RELATIONSHIP. She had the ability to enter a room and understand how everyone could be connected. She is a natural connector. She could put people from different spheres of life at ease. She had the ability to keep everyone close with a glance and a touch. She had a strong social media presence and thrived on her relationships. However, when people were not around she found it difficult to focus on herself and her own self-care. Compulsively overdoing her key essence of RELATIONSHIP by being "needy" was how she found CONNECTION externally and avoided feeling LONELY and ABANDONED.

Though she was at first slow to admit it, DYNAMISM was her third KEY ESSENCE. Initially she had found it difficult to admit her own natural charm—the idea that people were naturally drawn to her. She was a dazzler. Not just because she was physically beautiful, but also because she had a natural ability to hold people's attention. She was eloquent and able to sell any idea. But when the spotlight was not on her she seemed to lose energy. When out of the limelight she could not focus on fulfilling the promises she had made to others while holding center stage. Overdoing DYNAMISM by

holding center stage and over-committing was how she felt VISI-
BLE and HEARD, and avoided feeling INVISIBLE and IRREL-
EVANT. She was a "diva."

This part of our conversation had been difficult and challenging
for her. As we journeyed together, a fuller picture of Madra slowly
began to emerge as we identified her best essences and examined the
ways in which those essences became shadows of themselves.

GUIDEPOST 11.
DO THIS NOW
1. IDENTIFY YOUR KEY ESSENCES

*In the appendix to this book there is a list of 25
essences that make up the 25 cards I gave Madra. They are called,
the Essence Cards. Each essence is used as the basis of a personality
archetype. Each of the 25 archetypes is described in and out of balance. These descriptions have been updated and refined from the experiences of previous users. You do not need to relate to everything
in the description of a quality to choose it as one of your KEY ES-
SENCES.*

In your journal, note your answers to the following questions.

*1. Which three qualities would you say best describe you? These are
the ways you can't help being, for better or for worse. These three
essences are called your KEY ESSENCES. Your key essences are
the qualities you consistently experience. They are the qualities that
you and others would say best describe you for better or worse.*

Though they are what you like most about yourself, you tend to overdo them when you are stressed.

2. Read each description carefully. Identifying your key essences is not easy or comfortable. It will require honesty and courage. However, here's a tip: if you do not have an experience of currently OVERDOING the ESSENCE you choose, it is probably NOT your KEY ESSENCE at this time and should not be used as such.

KEY ESSENCE #1_____

KEY ESSENCE #2_____

KEY ESSENCE #3_____

3. When each key essence is in balance what do you do?

4. When each is overdone and goes out of balance, what do you do and what does it cost you and the people around you?

5. What do the people who know you best think about your choice of key essences? Do they agree that these are the three that best describe you for better or worse?

6. Which life-nutrients are you seeking when you overdo each of your key essences?

- ☐ *Voice*
- ☐ *Hope / Change*
- ☐ *Value / Visibility*
- ☐ *Connection / Relationship*
- ☐ *Safety / Belonging / Stability*

Remember, you don't have to get this perfectly the first time you do this exercise. Your insights and answers from working with this material will expand over time. Again, some of you might find it best to do these exercises with a close, trusted group of friends or advisors. However, once you've started the process of seriously asking these questions, these answers and insights will begin to work in you whether you are always conscious of it or not. This will be particularly true if you continue to practice the contemplative tools and affirmations in the previous chapters.

CHAPTER VII

BECOMING

~

CHARTING OUR UNIQUE INNER PATH
OF BALANCE

We actually don't fear change.

We crave it—just as long as it doesn't obliterate

our cherished identities. But real change

usually does.

W E ARE NOT STATIC BEINGS. We seem to always want
to find a new sense of balance and to grow. Though
we each have unique ways in which we find balance
and grow, it all starts from within.

Whatever we want to accomplish—whether to make more
money or to finally see a project to completion—underneath it all are
powerful DESIRES to grow. At the root of all of our wants and
needs are DESIRED ESSENCES. These are the essences that balance our KEY ESSENCES when those essences are overdone.

To desire is to re-member ourselves.

Remembering is the process of putting the pieces of our original selves back together and restoring our connection with vital life-nutrients. The physical accomplishments we want to have are harbingers of the aspects of ourselves that are being remembered and now need to be experienced.

Our KEY ESSENCES and DESIRED ESSENCES want to be expressed and integrated as part of our conscious identity and experience. They do this by inspiring challenging projects, goals, and dreams for our lives. This is the re-balancing and constant growth process that we experience. This internal growth process, if we are unaware of it, is the reason we often feel out of balance.

Below, I will walk us through an exercise to help us identify our DESIRED ESSENCES and our unique paths of BECOMING. This is an exercise we can master and repeat anytime we are feeling stuck. After we have mastered doing it for ourselves, I encourage us to do it with our loved ones, team members, and members of our tribes and communities. It will radically shift the way we see each other and what we can accomplish together.

GUIDEPOST 12.
DO THIS NOW
IDENTIFYING YOUR DESIRED ES-SENCES

What are the three essences (from the essences listed in the appendix) you have been saying to yourself BEFORE NOW that you wish to experience more? These are qualities that you do not seem to have a conscious experience of possessing yet consistently wish you did.

*DESIRED ESSENCE #1*_____

*DESIRED ESSENCE #2*_____

*DESIRED ESSENCE #3*_____

Madra's Desired Essences

As our sessions continued I asked Madra, "From the deck of the Essence Cards, which essences you wish to experience more of?"

She chose SELF-SUFFICIENCY, ORDER, and POWER.

"Why did you choose those qualities?" I asked her.

She said that she chose SELF-SUFFICIENCY because she wanted to be able to make her own way in the world powered by her own 'steam.' She had admired that quality in her sister who was independent of others and could pull on her own inner resources. ORDER was something she had been saying she needed: a better sense of discipline and timing. Her third desire, POWER is not an essence that most people choose easily. But she recalled picking it out at first glance from the deck.

"Why POWER?" I asked.

"Because I want to feel a sense of accomplishment."

THE PATH OF BECOMING

ALONG OUR PATHS TO OUR GOALS, desire is the catalyzing force—the force that pulls us toward a certain quality of life experience we want to have. That quality is often referred to generally as "life balance," but that can be further broken down into qualities such as FREEDOM, ABUNDANCE, JOY, ORDER, FOCUS, SIMPLICITY, PATIENCE etc.

No one starts out a journey to deliver their gifts, work at a job, or accomplish a life goal with the intention of destroying their relationships, finances, and sense of fun and exuberance in the process. No one says they want to get something done and self-destruct in the process. We have all seen how gifts delivered and goals pursued without balanced inner experiences often destroy those who accomplish them.

Too often the qualitative experiences we desire—our DESIRED ESSENCES—are not written into our goals and dreams. How many times have we arrived at our outward destination and not accomplished our inner journey?   Do we then feel as if we have to start all over again, or do we accept arriving without any experience of an inner evolution?

The quality of the experiences we want to have on our journey—qualities such as JOY, FREEDOM, FOCUS, STRENGTH, ORDER—exist as a counterpoint to the qualities we have mastered [KEY ESSENCES]. Together these qualities and essences form a path tailor-made just for us to experience. Along this path, we integrate the ESSENCES we have mastered [KEY ESSENCES] with essences that we now desire to experience more of [DESIRED ESSENCES]. We call this the Path of BECOMING.

Madra's Becoming

So along with the specific goals she had established for herself at the beginning of our time together, Madra wanted to experience:

IMAGINATION becoming POWER

RELATIONSHIP becoming SELF-SUFFICIENCY

DYNAMISM becoming ORDER

These are the ways in which she paired up her KEY ESSENCES & DESIRED ESSENCES.

GUIDEPOST 13.

DO THIS NOW

CREATE YOUR PATH OF BECOMING

List your KEY ESSENCES and DESIRED ESSENCES in the columns as indicated below. Place your Key Essences in order of their strength: how clearly you exhibit the qualities. Then list your Desired Essences in order of importance: the priorities you place on experiencing those qualities.

Key Essences   *Desired Essences*

_____   _____

_____   _____

_____   _____

Next, connect your Key Essences and Desired Essences based on your sense of which KEY ESSENCES compliment which DE-SIRED ESSENCES. To make these connections I recommend that you feel your way into them: do so intuitively. Listen to the internal tone each pairing creates in your body. Life knows where to flow to create the balance you need. You just have to listen carefully. Pair up each KEY ESSENCE with a DESIRED ESSENCE and as you do so, begin to notice how they correlate without your conscious choice

Key Essences		Desired Essences
_____	*becoming*	_____
_____	*becoming*	_____
_____	*becoming*	_____

PRACTICES ON THE PATH

OUR UNIQUE PATH TO BALANCE is the particular internal route we each take to get the LIFE-NUTRIENTS we need. Our path is tailor-made just for us based on our temperament and life challenges. It indicates how best we as individuals can find VOICE, HOPE, VISIBILITY, CONNECTION, and SAFETY. The path is not a list of things to do as much as it is the kind of qualitative experience we want to have.

GUIDEPOST 14.
DO THIS NOW
1. ESSENCE MEDITATION

After you have created these pathways to BECOMING do the following exercise each morning. For 25 minutes use the words of each of the pathways as a declaration and listen for the internal vibration of each word as it silently wakes up the internal quality and experience of the specific essences. For example, silently say: "I am IMAGINATION becoming POWER" and then sit silently for as long as you can, feeling the subtle sensations that the words awaken. When you can no longer feel the tone of the words, silently repeat the declaration again.

We will continue with this practice as we take steps towards accomplishing our goals. Along the way there are inner dragons we will have to slay. In the following chapters, we will meet our dragons and vanquish them.

THE FIVE DRAGONS
AT THE CROSSROADS

O UR KEY ESSENCES are the ways we have always known ourselves to be, for better or worse. We have seen how when stressed by difficult people or circumstances our KEY ESSENCES (or best qualities) become unbalanced caricatures of themselves. To bring them back into balance we must allow the alchemy between our KEY ESSENCES and our DESIRED ESSENCES—the qualities we now want to experience—to be realized. When these are brought together we will begin to sense an inner PATH TO BECOMING. This is the path of inner balance where we begin to feel more grounded, hear our own voice, sense our value, and move forward confidently.

However, as we begin to walk along this path there are emotional dragons that we have heretofore avoided, but which we now must consciously slay.

Madra's Dragons

That morning I prepared for my meeting with Madra by taking a look at the three KEY ESSENCES she had chosen from the deck of the Essence Cards. These were the three qualities that she said described her "to a fault." They were the qualities she could not help but display for better or worse.

I began with this question: *"When you overdo IMAGINA-TION what are you trying to AVOID feeling?"*

"I have to think about this," Madra said, and then repeated, *"When I over-do IMAGINATION what am I trying to avoid feeling?"*

"I really want you consider this. IMAGINATION is an essence primarily associated with the element FIRE. This is the element that allows for visibility and insight. When it is overdone by fantasizing new ideas constantly, it can indicate a fear of shaming, rejection, or invisibility. When you do this your imagination becomes a mask that makes everything look good. The essence IMAGINATION is also secondarily associated with NATURE. This is the element that allows things to grow. So, when imagination is overdone it is also often a strategy to avoid feeling stuck and to make us feel that things are moving when they actually are not."

"So, when I overdo RELATIONSHIPS—by being a needy so-cialite—what feeling am I trying to avoid feeling?" she muttered.

"What is the PRIMARY element that RELATIONSHIP describes I asked her?"

Flipping the water card over, she whispered, *"WATER."*

"RELATIONSHIP is an essence primarily associated with the

element WATER, the element of CONNECTION," I added.

"I am avoiding LONELINESS and ABANDONMENT," she whispered.

"Talk to me about your feelings of loneliness and abandonment," I gently asked.

"It's hard to talk about, but when I was about five my mother went away and left me with an aunt..."

THE QUALITIES THAT are our KEY ESSENCES are qualities that we chose much earlier on in life, when we first had experiences in which we were consciously wounded—made to feel silenced, hopeless, invisible, abandoned, or dislocated at a deep level. We chose our KEY ESSENCES in an effort to survive our human journey through some of the earliest stages of our lives. For example, we may choose SELF-SUFFICIENCY when we are made to feel abandoned and without the ability to advocate for ourselves. This happens when a child grows up in a home in which other children are given preferential treatment, such as gifts or being taken out, while the abandoned child is left at home. The choice to become SELF-SUFFICIENT is a reaction to the pain of abandonment and silencing. The child will keep choosing this quality when difficult people and circumstances, or challenging projects and goals trigger old, painful emotions of ABANDONMENT. This will be how that child comes to know herself: as someone who is independent, resourceful, or SELF-SUFFICIENT. People who know her well will describe it as her best quality. But when faced with difficulty, she will often not ask for help. She will prefer to tough it out rather than seek the help of friends or colleagues. The result will be the loss of resources available in her community or at work, and her friends and colleagues will feel when they are unable to contribute to her and her projects.

If we are to find new inner spaces of balance from which to grow and offer gifts to the world, we must slay the emotional dragons that we have avoided.

Often, we arrive at an outward destination having accomplished a tremendous goal and yet have no sense of fulfillment. This happens when we have relied heavily on our strengths, donned our favorite mask, and toughed it out. We did what we know works, but in the process destroyed relationships and our own well-being. This happens when we do not also take a conscious inner journey to confront our fears.

I remember being the chief architect of the founding declaration of the first gathering of the International Black Summit in Atlanta. I had taken the initiative to draft the declaration with careful note-taking and headed up a group tasked with its preparation. In the end, I gave up my role in the final draft proposal in what had become a freewheeling process with many players. I left the meeting because I could not control things. I did so grudgingly and exhausted from having to defend my point of view. When the draft declaration was presented at the conference, edited and approved, I stood on the platform with the team and we were applauded. When I was singled out and heard people acknowledging me for my work I was, however, unable to receive their outpouring of love. I had no clue what they were acknowledging me for. I stood there unable to connect with them or see myself. I had not consciously slayed my dragons: my fear of losing control, value, and visibility. I had not consciously stepped through those fears into a freeing experience of creativity. There was nothing that I had consciously chosen to conquer.

The same feeling of non-accomplishment happens when we sense that we have been going in a circle, repeating the same experiences over and over. This happens because in the course of pursuing our goals we did not take the inner paths where our DRAGON-FEARS live. When we consciously take this inner journey, we will have the heads of our dragons to show.

THE FIVE DRAGONS OF FEAR

THESE DRAGONS STAND at the crossroads between our KEY ESSENCES—how we have known ourselves, for better or worse, and our DESIRED ESSENCES—the essences we now desire to experience more of. These dragons guard over the SHADOW side of our KEY ESSENCES—STRENGTH that can become murderous, IMAGINATION relegated to dreaming, and DYNAMISM reduced to spotlight grabbing "divadom." They define the places where we choose to retreat or press on, only to repeat past results. They walk the dividing line between "me" and "them," "this" and "that."

The Crossroads

KEY ESSENCE

THIS   THEM

PAST   FUTURE

ME   THAT

DESIRED ESSENCE

Each dragon is triggered at "the crossroads" of our lives - at difficult
stages:

- ℵ When we are executing challenging projects and
  are unsure of the next steps
- ℵ When we are dealing with change that shatters
  our sense of self
- ℵ When we must become more transparent and
  visible for the things we say we believe in
- ℵ When we have difficult requests to make of
  others, or must face difficult people in our lives
- ℵ When we need to bring order to chaos

At the crossroads of our lives we are pulled by the shadows of our

KEY ESSENCES—the qualities we possess for better or worse; while our DESIRED ESSENCES—the qualities we want to experience more of—are like distant dreams. It is at the crossroads—these pivotal moments of choice in our lives—where we lose touch with the present moment and look back to the past for direction and imagine a future in order to provide a salve for our present dilemma. Yet, both the past and the future are unreal. It is here that our world is divided into "ME" versus "THEM," this and that, and each of the five *Complaints of the Ego* dominate our thinking. It is here that we try to fix the behaviors of others or manipulate situations by changing our behavior in order to fix someone or something.

But at the crossroads the only thing that is real is the present moment. It is here that we must confront the dragon-fears that keep us stuck if we are to step into the truly self-transformative opportunity of the moment—our BECOMING. It is at these crossroads, seemingly cut off from our inner connection with life's nutrients—our source of well-being and balance—that the price of reconnection must be paid. The cost of our BECOMING is the heads of our dragons.

Below are the five dragon-fears at the root of our experience at these crossroads that we must confront and slay. I have listed them this time with their relationship to each one of the five elements. Knowing the elemental associations of our specific emotional triggers will be helpful, as in the coming chapters we begin to:

- ✗ See how these fears are triggered by the people around us
- ✗ Design nature-based ritual-practices to help us heal from our wounds and locate new inner experiences of balance
- ✗ Identify where in our physical body these fears reside

MINERAL

UN-HEARD & IRRELEVANT

The fear we feel when our unique point of view has been excluded, when our unique story is not heard. The feeling of irrelevance. This fear disconnects us from MINERAL, the elemental nutrient that gives us our VOICE.

NATURE

HOPELESSNESS & STAGNATION

The fear we feel when we believe that the things and people around us will not change or grow, that we are stuck and no longer in control. This fear disconnects us from the element of NATURE, the elemental nutrient that allows things to change and evolve.

FIRE

INVISIBILITY/WORTHLESSNESS

The fear we feel when we are not seen or valued, the feeling of worthlessness. This fear disconnects us from FIRE, the elemental nutrient that makes it possible for us to see our value to the world.

WATER

LONELINESS & ABANDONMENT

The fear we feel when we are isolated and abandoned. This fear disconnects us from the elemental nutrient WATER which connects us peacefully and freely to others.

EARTH

HOMELESSNESS & VULNERABILITY

The fear we feel when we are dislocated, when things are unsafe, chaotic, and unbalanced. This fear disconnects us from EARTH, the elemental nutrient that provides us with a sense of security and belonging.

These fears stand in the way of us getting the ESSENTIAL NU-TRIENTS we need for life balance. These are the feelings that we avoid at all cost. Rather than feel these things we prefer to mask our best qualities and, in that process, destroy our health, wreck our finances, break up our relationships, dismember our communities, and conceal our truth.

THE CHOICE AT THE CROSSROADS

SO HERE WE ARE, going merrily along and life throws us a snag—a big project we don't know how to do, a difficult person, a health challenge, a large request that we have to make, the choice to work at what we love or earn money for our survival. The crossroad is the place where we tend to procrastinate, hobbled by the fear of the loss of our identity, or a change in the circumstances that now keep us secure. This upheaval will jeopardize the comfort of our current relationships, bringing us face-to-face with rejection. We will confront hopelessness, run the risk of not being heard or understood, and make embarrassing mistakes. The crossroad is where we meet life's dilemmas. It is where we try to balance life, but too often attempt to do so externally.

At the crossroad, we can choose to:

ℵ   Blame the difficult people in our lives for having brought us to this point and create arguments

ℵ   Have yet another meeting

ℵ   Issue another memo with unclear objectives

- ℵ Fail to communicate effectively with the people in our families or on our teams
- ℵ Become a control freak
- ℵ Become a martyr to the cause
- ℵ Become an attacker and chop off heads
- ℵ Become silent and malicious
- ℵ Just stand there and wait for something to happen

At the crossroads there is also a choice to say YES to our new BECOMING.

At the crossroads of life, we think that we are presented with an either/or choice. Either we do this or we do that. Do we stop communicating or do we say what's in our thoughts? Do we stay or do we go? Should we risk taking the leap or stay put? But what if these were not our real choices? What if the crossroads is instead an opportunity to inwardly say "Yes" to the inner experiences of STRENGTH, SUFFICIENCY, and POWER that we have DESIRED?

At the crossroads, the primary choices aren't really about what to do, but rather what to allow ourselves to feel, experience, and become. It is at the crossroads that we find balance and growth. The desires we have and the goals we want to accomplish are on the other side of the feelings we are trying to avoid.

The choice to say "Yes" at the crossroads to the pursuit of balance and growth is not the easiest choice to make. It has no guarantee of comfort and will bring us into direct confrontation with our fears. Yet this inner experience of our BECOMING is the salve to any emotional wounds that we carry within us. The alchemy of our pain and this new feeling about who we are BECOMING creates a powerful vibrational pathway that attracts the kinds of people and circumstances towards us that will allow for unimagined possibilities. As we carry this feeling of BECOMING around with us in our daily life it will help us sense what to do next in each situation because we will know what strengthens this feeling and what diminishes it. This sense of knowing right direction and right action will allow for a new sense of integrity, one founded not just on following rules and accessing the pros and cons, but on following the path of our heart.

MEET YOUR DRAGONS

AS WE NOTED ABOVE, each ESSENCE in the deck of ESSENCE CARDS is associated with one or more elements. When a KEY ESSENCE is overdone, it points to the specific emotion that is being avoided—the DRAGON which we must now confront in order to step into the experience of balance and growth we have long desired.

When we experience the fears our dragons represent with complete awareness, the fears dissolve. This may be hard to believe but it is true. Because immediately underneath these fears are the deeper DESIRED ESSENCES that are seeking to be expressed. When we allow those DESIRED ESSENCES to be expressed they merge with our KEY ESSENCES, dissolving the shadows of our KEY ESSENCES and thereby empowering us to experience ourselves in new and amazing ways.

Let's face our dragons together!

GUIDEPOST 15.

DO THIS NOW

1. For each of your KEY ESSENCES (taken one at a time) complete the following sentence:

"When I overdo my KEY ESSENCE I do so in order to AVOID feeling _____."

- ☐ *Unheard / Irrelevant / Silenced*
- ☐ *Hopeless / Stuck / Stagnant / Out of Control*
- ☐ *Invisible / Worthless / Rejected*
- ☐ *Abandoned / Lonely / Betrayed*
- ☐ *UNSAFE / Chaotic / Defenseless*

2. Take a look at the ESSENCE CARDS that represent each of your KEY ESSENCES. [See the table of essences in the appendix.] What is the primary ELEMENT of that essence? Is it MINERAL, NATURE, FIRE, WATER, or EARTH?

Note:

- א *MINERAL ESSENCES when overdone seek to avoid being silenced*
- א *NATURE ESSENCES when overdone seek to avoid hopelessness, feeing stuck or out of control*
- א *FIRE ESSENCES when overdone seek to avoid invisibility, worthlessness, and rejection*
- א *WATER ESSENCES when overdone seek to avoid*

abandonment and betrayal

א   *EARTH ESSENCES when overdone seek to avoid feel-ing unsafe, dislocated, or homeless*

3. Spend time journaling any insights gained from the above quiz. Begin to take a closer look at how each of your KEY ESSENCES goes out of balance. • When each goes out of balance, what do you do?

א   *Why? What are you trying to avoid feeling?*

א   *What does it cost you?*

א   *What does it cost others?*

This exercise will challenge you deeply. These are the difficult questions that we avoid since they take us into the dungeons where our dragons live. If we are to find a new sense of inner balance we must enter that dungeon and shine a light on our dragons in order to diminish their power over us.

In the following chapters, we will be introduced to powerful practices for keeping ourselves in balance in the face of our greatest fears, those often triggered by members of our tribe—the people closest to us.

But first, please complete the exercise above.

CHAPTER IX

OUR TRIBE

N O ONE EXISTS ALONE –though it can sometimes feel that way. When we look closer at the crossroads—the places of transition where we make our most critical decisions—we are not there alone. We exist with others as lovers, co-workers and friends, people in our businesses, community organizations, families, and political movements. It is these people who are close to us who more often than not trigger our dragon-fears.

Our sense of balance and fulfillment is experienced not only as an expression of our own self-awareness and BECOMING, but also as an expression of the quality of our relationships with others. The quality of those relationships is an expression of our acceptance of the people in our lives.

Our acceptance of others will involve taking a deep look at the people closest or most impactful to us and taking the first steps to understand where they are and where we are in relationship to them.

This will mean gaining insights into why they do the things they do: their KEY ESSENCES, their fears, how they too have been wounded and their shadows. Most importantly, if we are to exist peacefully and grow together, we need to gain a sense of the Path of BECOMING upon which we are each walking.

It is wonderful when this work is done together in a group. I have seen friends sit with the Essence Cards talking and learning about each other deep into the night. Though they have been good friends, they heard from each other stories that had been kept hidden, laughed with each other over the essences and shadows they shared, and grew in compassion and understanding of each other.

Often however, the work of acceptance has to be done alone. This is the case when others are not interested in doing the work or where the relationship is in conflict.

We can only come to accept others after doing this work for ourselves. This is necessary if we are to act with awareness and find new balance.

Below I will share some tools for growing our awareness of ourselves and the people around us.

THE ELEMENTS IN OUR TRIBE

BASIC TO OUR UNDERSTANDING of the elemental dynamics that come into play within ANY group is awareness of the elemental make-up of the individuals who comprise the group or tribe—the people who form our circle. Each person in our tribe, including the difficult ones, represents the activity of one of the five elements.

The element that person is most associated with will let you know an important driver behind their actions and behaviors.

The information that follows is not intended to negate other insightful tools such as one's "astrological sign" or "personality type" that derive from some other wonderful matrices that exist. What follows is an additional tool with which to grow our awareness of ourselves and others. It is a simple tool that comes from the Dagara tradition in West Africa as taught to me by Elder Malidoma Patrice Somé. I share it with you here because it has been invaluable in helping me to understand and make peace with others. I have used it extensively in my work.

To identify the element associated with an individual, you must know the last digit of their birth year.

א MINERAL PEOPLE are born in the
  years ending in 4 or 9

א NATURE PEOPLE are born in the years
  ending in 3 or 8

א FIRE PEOPLE are born in the years
  ending in 2 or 7

א WATER PEOPLE are born in the years
  ending in 1 or 6

א EARTH PEOPLE are born in the years
  ending in 0 or 5.

MINERAL PEOPLE

These are the folks that help us make sense of things. They want to find the narrative or the logic in all things. They are storytellers and communicators. They are emotionally triggered by feeling irrelevant or unheard.

NATURE PEOPLE

Nature people are engaged in an ongoing quest for change. They often seem to be boundless in their ability to initiate and be curious about things. They tend to be free-spirited and cannot be contained. They are known for their strange and odd ways of doing things. They are spontaneous and magical. They are emotionally vulnerable to feeling stuck or not in control.

FIRE PEOPLE

These are the people who bring hidden things to light. They are expressive people. Others can feel burnt by their delivery and insight. They are creators, they tend to initiate and make things happen. They are emotionally triggered by feelings of invisibility.

WATER PEOPLE

These people are often the ones who bring people together to resolve conflict, soothe things over, and make peace and reconciliation. They are compassionate and feel things deeply. They are emotionally vulnerable to abandonment and betrayal.

EARTH PEOPLE

Earth people are very much concerned with the care and well-being of the community or group. Caring and protecting forms the central thrust of most of what they do. They are emotionally vulnerable to disorder and instability.

GUIDEPOST 16.
DO THIS NOW

1. *Identify your own element association or Element TRIBE.*

2. *Among your friends, coworkers, and family begin to identify each person's element association. Begin to notice:*

> א *The contribution that each person's elemental nature makes to your life and the life of the tribe.*

   ℵ *The challenge that the person's elemental association represents for you or the tribe*

   ℵ *If you are working in a team, begin to notice how the team is elementally configured. What element is there in abundance? What element is missing?*

TRIBAL ROLES

THE PEOPLE AROUND US move in and out of five distinct roles. This is true regardless of whether these roles are within the context of a family, workplace, or social gathering. These roles are not fixed as one person can embody more than one role in your life. Each role is distinguished by one of the five elements. Here are the tribal roles.

MINERAL

STORYTELLERS

These are the people who through their stories—their art and voice—inspire and give meaning to our lives. They include artists and novelists, historians and poets. They could also include parental and familial deceased who played important roles in our development. These individuals who have passed on are of particular relevance because their transformations—finished and unfinished—open narrative pathways for our journey ahead. Ancestors become more relevant as players in our lives depending upon our closeness to them. They pass on the genetic blueprint for our lives. There are more complete bodies of work around family constellations that look more deeply at these mechanics than I can here. I mention it in this chapter so that we can have a full picture of the roles of the people in our lives—living and deceased—and how they help shape the narratives we have adopted about our lives.

NATURE

ELDERS

These are the people in our lives that pass on instruction, experiential knowledge, and know-how. They have the ability to help us unblock limited perceptions. They inspire and cause us to imagine ourselves in new ways and to dream of new possibilities.

FIRE

HUNTERS & WARRIORS

Our hunters are our cheerleaders. They are the people who go out and spread the good news about who we are and what we are up to. They come back to us with resources and new relationships that will help us to move forward. Our warriors are the difficult people in our lives.

These are the people who know how to push our buttons, how

to trigger emotions that we have tried to avoid. Sometimes there are people who are both hunters and warriors. Warriors appear at the crossroads when we are about to make big decisions about the direction of our lives.

WATER

HEALERS

These are the people in our lives who understand how to keep things moving along. They include our life coaches as well as personal and professional advisors. They know living systems and ways of negotiating that keep things progressing.

EARTH

CHILDREN

These are the people in our lives to whom we give. They are the ones that come to us and ask us to be around to guide and nurture them.

GIFTING & RECEIVING GIFTS

OUR TRIBES are where we source and express the life-nutrient CON-NECTION. It is in our tribes that we connect to others by giving and receiving the GIFTS of our ESSENCE. The refusal to give and receive these gifts within our tribes is often a source of conflict and misunderstanding. The tribe, like the biological family, is understood through the element of water. Water is what connects us and allows for fluidity. When our gifts are not allowed to flow, there is coldness on the one hand and anger on the other.

Each of us has gifts to offer. What are the gifts that we have for the people around us? What gifts are they giving us? Have we received them? Have we acknowledged receiving them? Have our gifts been acknowledged?

By now we may have begun to wonder about the KEY ESSENCES and DESIRED ESSENCES of the people closest to us. It is hard not to wonder about this as our attention is drawn to behaviors in others that show the patterns of ESSENCES we have become familiar with—in and out of balance. In this chapter, we will have an opportunity to begin to deepen our awareness of the KEY ESSENCES & DESIRED ESSENCES of the people closest to us. Begin to wonder about others. What are their KEY ESSENCES? What are their DESIRED ESSENCES?

If you can, ask them to choose those from the list of 25 Essences.

We each model our KEY and DESIRED ESSENCES for each other, both their positive aspects and their shadows. For example, warriors often behave in ways that express the shadow side of an essence we desire. This happens when you desire FOCUS and your partner, unconcerned about your feelings, is simply focused on the next step. You can criticize him for his lack of compassion, or notice that he brings you the gift of FOCUS, albeit packaged in a way that makes you uncomfortable. Often the warrior helps reveal for us DE-SIRED ESSENCES that we were not consciously aware of having. Conversely, they can reveal the shadows of our KEY ESSENCES that we have not accepted.

Unpacking these gifts and recognizing how they are being brought or given is critical if we are to be at peace. We could spend a lifetime trying to make sense of the difficult people in our lives. If we fail to acknowledge their gifts, we rob ourselves of presence and abundance.

The following process is intended to help us uncover these gifts, acknowledge them, and free ourselves to be more deeply present to the unfolding of our BECOMING and the role of the people around us in that process.

GUIDEPOST 17.
DO THIS NOW
BEGIN TO JOURNAL ABOUT THE FOL-LOWING:

1. After choosing an artist, poet, or writer whom you admire or an ancestor to whom you were close while they were alive, ask yourself the following questions: What are their KEY ESSENCES and DE-SIRES? Do you share any in common, and if so which? What did they say, or are they saying to you, that you have been unwilling to hear?

2. After choosing an ELDER to whom you are closest ask yourself the following questions: What are your Elder's KEY ESSENCES and *DESIRES? What are the essences and desires you share with this ELDER? How are they expressed? In what ways can you see that they have been consciously or unconsciously asking you to change?*

3a. Your CHEERLEADERS are the people who champion your causes, who believe in you. Choose one and answer this question: Which of your essences and desires do they share? Have you acknowledged their value in demonstrating for you the qualities you desire?

3b. Your WARRIORS will be dealt with separately at the end of this chapter.

4. ADVISORS/SHAMAN: These are the people around you who help you to see patterns and cycles; they help you avoid pitfalls. In what ways have they been asking you to be connected to the people and things around you?

5. CHILDREN. These are the people around you who look up to you; they are the people whom you lead and inspire. Which of your KEY ESSENCES do you think most inspire them? What are they asking from you that would make them feel safe? What are the qualities and experiences that you have not provided?

THE GIFT OF THE WARRIOR

LET'S SPEND SOME TIME focusing on our WARRORS—the difficult people in our lives. Warriors often have an ESSENCE that we DESIRE. Often though they express this quality in a seemingly unbalanced way such that we experience the shadow side of the ESSENCE we desire. Or, they exhibit the shadow of one of our KEY

ESSENCES that we have not been willing to accept. This is what triggers us. We can see ourselves in them and wish they could also embody some of our best qualities or KEY ESSENCES. In this way, they present to us a fractured and upsetting image of our own ESSENCES.

Often though our WARRIOR sees in us a KEY ESSENCE that he or she has been desiring, which we sometimes display in an unbalanced way. We both have gifts to give each other!

Our warriors offer challenging relationships. They are like the "dazzlers" who keeps us mesmerized yet are unable to fulfill their promise, the "know it alls," the "control freaks," the "dreamers." These difficult people appear in our lives to reflect aspects of ourselves, our own shadows of which we are often unaware. Again, these shadows can be unbalanced KEY ESSENCES that we have, but of which we are unconscious. Once we become aware that these are reflections of unseen aspects of ourselves, we can begin the process of healing for ourselves and our relationships.

We each have cosmic appointments with each other: gifts and messages to deliver, paths to help each other navigate, new ideas to express that will shape the beauty of our world. However, most of our communications are in the unsaid though, in the silences, in the recognition of the inner pathways we open for each other. When we speak perhaps all there is to say is, "I see you. Thank you. I hear you. You have inspired my growth. We are one. We are here."

What are the ESSENCES of our WARRIORS? What KEY ESSENCES or DESIRED ESSENCES do we share if any? What are the shared or different ways in which our KEY ESSENCES go out of balance? When our KEY ESSENCES go out of balance what LIFE-NUTRIENTS are we each trying to experience and what fears are we each trying to avoid feeling?

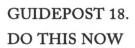

GUIDEPOST 18.
DO THIS NOW
Completing Relationships

Sometimes it is difficult to see the gift that our most difficult relationships bring. Oftentimes these relationships seem devoid of any sense of generosity. On the surface, there is very little in the way of value that is being given or received. The sense of imbalance in our relationships steals our attention. When our attention wanders, we are not present to the flow of abundance that is present in the relationship. Completing relationships through communication—providing what is needed to right the imbalance—through communication is a practice that restores balance and reciprocity.

Begin to ask yourself: Where in my life do I have a sense of owing someone:

1. A hearing, a moment to truly be listened to

2. An acknowledgement of their courage in the face of their unique challenge

3. A "thank you," an acknowledgment or expression of gratitude for their presence

4. Companionship and compassion

5. An apology

This path is not an easy path. It will require attention over a number of cycles, and deepening our awareness of each ESSENCE and how those ESSENCES manifest in our own behaviors and the actions of the people around us. As we go further along this path it will bring us a sense of gratitude for each and every person around us, for their beauty and the gifts we each possess.

CHAPTER X

KEY INNER PRACTICES FOR SLAYING OUR DRAGONS

O UR DRAGON-FEARS WILL BE ENCOUNTERED at the transformational crossroads of our lives—where we will encounter our warriors while completing a challenging project, having a difficult conversation, navigating changing roles in a relationship, negotiating our value, or stepping into unknown territory. At a crossroad, our existing identity—the way we know ourselves—is not big enough for us to hold the opportunities or possibilities being presented, so we squander resources and let time slip by. This is the case when, for example, for an unknown reason we lose a big check that was given as a gift to help pursue a dream. This is called a "crisis of having." Here our identity is not big enough to hold what we have and the possibilities presented. So, we lose things, give our power away, make bad decisions, procrastinate, get together with the wrong people, and don't follow up. When this happens our memory of ourselves needs to be refreshed. The crossroads is where our identity is transformed.

When we are at the crossroads the following three practices will be helpful. Once we have identified the specific fears to which we are vulnerable, we can begin to incorporate them into our lives on a daily basis. [Note: If you have not completed the exercise in the last chapter to identify the unique dragon-fears to which you are vulnerable, go back and do so now.]

These practices are designed to help us slay our dragons, as it is these dragons that cause us to restrict our sense of ourselves and what we can accomplish. Use the practices separately, progressively—one after the other—or combine them with each other. Expand on them or use them to re-create your own existing practices. These practices are not intended to be exhaustive or limiting. However, each of the three practices below provides a powerful set of basics for confronting our fears directly.

1. THE PRACTICE OF GRATITUDE & ALLOWING

ALL THOUGHTS, EMOTIONS, and attitudes except those coming from GRATITUDE have been acquired since birth. They were nurtured. Gratitude, on the other hand, is our natural way of being. It is the first and most important ritual to invoke when at a crossroad.

It is by ALLOWING that we negotiate and survive (and even

thrive) on change. Everything changes in order to reveal that which does not. ALLOWING is not passivity or agreement. It actively involves transforming what is being felt and experienced into a new place from which to BECOME.

Whether we are aware of it or not we are always BECOMING. In this book, I have sought to bring this underlying current of our experience to our conscious awareness. GRATITUDE & ALLOWING are the tools that connect the changing internal and external expressions of our BECOMING. GRATITUDE & ALLOWING make it possible for us to experience life and its circumstances as expressions of our BECOMING, regardless of appearances.

As we BECOME sometimes life will flow easily; at other times, there can be great upheavals. This practice of GRATITUDE & ALLOWING will help us to accept our experiences and to respond from a place of balance and power. It is the practice that unites the inner and outer worlds of our experience. It is like the water of libation that is poured to symbolize our connection with the unseen. This practice is in the tears and greeting exchanged between the prodigal son and the father on the son's "return to home." With this practice, "otherness" dissolves. It knits dimensions together so we can feel our connection to places, people, and things. It is the mantra of union.

When we invoke gratitude & ALLOWING at the crossroads of our lives all seeming choices evaporate, leaving a singular path of BECOMING upon which we can move forward freely in grace. This is the practice that opens the way.

There is a saying: "Whatever you let be, let's you be." Whenever we are at a crossroads, we must:

1. Make ourselves consciously aware of the activity in our bodies, our circumstances, and the people in our environment. As you do this, suspend any judgments or analysis of yourself or what's happening.

2. Remember our Path of BECOMING creates new narratives about our circumstances, ones that align with who we are becoming. You can find these narratives by asking: how does this situation help me to experience more of who I am BECOMING?

3. Center ourselves with this simple thought: "Gratefully, I let it be."

2. A Silent Meditation Practice

As an introduction to this practice, let me open with the following quote.

> *"The aim of practice is not to develop an attitude which allows a man to acquire a state of harmony and peace wherein nothing can ever trouble him. On the contrary, practice should teach him to let himself be assaulted, perturbed, moved, insulted, broken, and battered—that is to say, it should enable him to dare to let go of his futile hankering after harmony, surcease of*

pain, and a comfortable life in order that he may discover, in doing battle with the forces that oppose him, that which awaits him beyond the world of opposites. The first necessity is that we should have the courage to face life and encounter all that is most perilous in the world. When this is possible, meditation itself becomes the means by which we accept and welcome the demons which arise from the unconscious... Only if we venture repeatedly through zones of annihilation, can our contact with Divine Being, which is beyond annihilation, become firm and stable. The more a man learns whole-heartedly to confront the world that threatens him with isolation, the more are the depths of the Ground of Being revealed and the possibilities of new life and Becoming opened."

~ THE WAY OF TRANSFORMATION ~ KARLFRIED GRAF
VON DURCKHEIM

SILENCE is the FIRST ESSENCE. It is the first letter, so to speak in the alphabet of the language of our deepest Self. It is the essence from which all others unfold. The aim of the practice of silent meditation is to deepen our awareness of and connection to the silent Source of Life that flows from within. In meditation, we greet that Source and become one with it. This Source is the home of all the ESSENCES. This Source is active in every atom in the body. It emits a silent vibration that powers our breath and the fires and currents that create and vitalize each organ of our bodies.

Our mind, trained to be externally focused, thinks itself separate from this Source. Triggered by sensed circumstances of the present, memories of the past or an imagined future, it chatters on even during meditation. This chatter affects the quality of our emotions, mental images, and the energy stream that creates and vitalizes our bodies. As our practice deepens our ability to stay focused on the seamless, inner, invisible Source—the home of our essential nature— becomes stronger. Gradually we will begin to identify ourselves as this Source—as our essential SELF. This is the intention of meditation—to realize our oneness with the SELF and to experience our bodies, lives, and the world as a manifestation of that SELF.

Here are five elementally-calibrated steps to support our silent meditation practice. They will help us to face the chatter and to accept and transform the dragon-fears that arise from the unconscious during meditation and ultimately in our day-to-day lives.

Preparing for Meditation

Sit comfortably with your back straight; don't tuck your chin. Sit on a chair if you need to. However you sit, create as much space as possible between your limbs and your body. Rest your arms gently on your knees with your palms up and fingers loose and open.

STEP 1

PHYSICAL SENSATION

Begin to allow yourself to feel the activity of the body from the inside. Remember 99.9 % of the body is empty space. This space is home to the essential self. This space permeates the body and out of it comes every atom, cell, tissue, and organ. Imagine that you are that space—centered in the body yet existing everywhere.

Simply allow yourself to feel the sensations in your body without naming them. These may be sensations of tightness or expansion, tingling, stinging, heat, or numbness. Feel them. Allow them to be. Use your awareness to search actively for all the sensations in your body. Take each area of the body one by one. Surround each sensation with your awareness and make space for them to be as they are. In other words, don't try to change them, to make them go away, or to hold onto them. Experience each sensation as a physical phenomenon. It is these sensations that the inner Self experiences as it continuously births itself into existence. To the Self, birth and rebirth are nameless activities—just part of the process of manifestation. From the point of view of the mind, looking out with its externalized focus on survival, these sensations are experienced as waves of annihilation that threaten its existence. One mind may experience them as birthing; another as dying. In meditation, we get to choose our experience of life. I recommend that we try not to name these sensations, judge, or analyze them. As I mentioned earlier, "Whatever you let be, lets you be."

STEP 2.

EMOTION

Begin to notice the movement of emotions in your body. There is no need to try to name them. At the crossroads, there is a powerful stew of emotions that can make us feel "good" or "bad." These emotions are like waves. They are more fluid than physical sensations. They tend to feel like waves swelling up or rivers roaming through the body. Allow yourself to experience each wave or river. Notice this, as it is, without trying to change any of it in an attempt to feel better. Feel them swell as waves and then dissipate. Feel them swell from small ripples into big waves. Sometimes you will feel like you are drowning; let yourself go under. Remain still and observant. Again, the Self experiences all this as nameless activity—part of the process of manifestation. Again, from the point of view of the mind, looking out with its externalized focus on survival, these sensations are experienced as waves of annihilation that threaten its existence. One experiences them as birthing, the other experiences them as dying. Choose.

STEP 3

THOUGHTS

During stillness simply notice the thoughts that enter your awareness. At the crossroads, there is a heady mix of thoughts. Essentially these are the Five Complaints of the Ego, explored in Chapter III. It is here in this mind-fire that we come up with ways to fix ourselves and others, try to figure things out, attempt to identify who or what is affecting us, blame others for our situation, tell ourselves that we are not good enough or that we are not doing things right, or convince ourselves of what we really deserve. Notice that attached to each thought are emotional waves and physical sensations. Become aware of the connections. Again, the Self experiences all this as nameless activity—part of the process of its birthing. From the point of view of the mind, looking out with its externalized focus on survival, these thoughts are essential for its survival. One experiences these thoughts as part of the process of creation, the other experiences them as a life and death debate about the survival of its self-concept. Choose.

STEP 4

TIME BASED IMAGES

Next, notice the future projections and pictures of the past that your mind is creating. Simply observe them. Begin to notice where your thinking is focused. It will either be in the past or the future. The dilemma at the crossroads—the choice to move or remain stuck—will send you to the past where you have stored the memories of past wounds. You will gather those memories and project them as pictures of what might happen "if." At the crossroads, we tend to walk back and forth in our minds between our version of the past and future projections. This motion is what gives us the experience of being stuck. Notice how these time-based images influence your thoughts, emotions, and physical sensations.

STEP 5

IDENTITY

Keep still and go deeper. Continue to be aware of what is showing up to you as the thoughts, emotions, and sensations within you. In each sensation, thought, emotion, and image you will experience in meditation there is an implicit embedded identity. The voice of that identity usually starts with "I AM…" For example, "I AM TIRED.

I AM AFRAID. I AM HURT. I AM BETRAYED. I AM NOT
DOING THIS RIGHT..." Be aware of that identity. Simply observe.

Enter the Silence

Throughout all five steps notice your tendency to want to enter the
fray with "positive" affirmations, self-counseling, mediating, strate-
gizing, or pep talks. As you successfully resist this temptation SI-
LENCE will emerge. SILENCE is the FIRST ESSENCE. It is the
one from which all others unfold. Listen for it. It is there. Give it
your full attention. Do not name it. Do not see it as the thing that's
going to make everything go away and fix everything. Simply be
aware of it. Once you locate it do not try to give it anything to do.
Simply give it your attention for as long as possible. Do not try to
increase it or hold on to it. It does not need your help. Simply give it
your attention and allow it to be. If distracted, simply observe the
thought, emotion, or sensation that has distracted you; listen again
for the silence and again give it your full attention. The silence will
expand with attention. With new awareness, allow the silence and its
vibration to be experienced.

A Word on the Breath

The breath is a product of and a fuel for the activity of creation by all
of the 25 ESSENCES that make up the ESSENTIAL Self. We actually don't breathe. We are breathed. This is why we can't stop our
breath except for short periods of time. What we can do though is

cooperate with our breath as co-creators. We can join in with its activity. We can greet and welcome each breath and amplify it by allowing it, making room in our bodies for it, by breathing deeply, allowing it to come all the way in and allowing it to be exhaled all the way out. We do not need to force the breath. We must simply stay with it and mirror it as a co-creative activity with our ESSENTIAL Self.

In meditation begin to notice the space out of which your breath arises. Consciously feel for it. Feel it as it expands and contracts, and allow your body to expand and contract with it.

Stilling the Mind

Often, I hear people say, "When I am meditating, I cannot get my mind to be still." You too may be asking what's happening when the mind wanders during meditation. Let's take a moment to address this now.

First, the purpose of meditation is not to silence the process of thinking. The purpose of meditation is to realize our oneness with our Essential Self—who we really are—as the space in which all the Essences reside, and from which our lives, including our mind and its thoughts, unfold. This is accomplished by expanding our awareness, or the content of our consciousness, until oneness is realized. Meditation can be said to be the process of expanding our conscious experience of ourselves, or as some say: our consciousness. To accomplish this, our focusing mechanisms are our attention and will.

During meditation, the thinking mind is just one thing for our consciousness to be aware of. There are also the comings in and go-ings out of the breath, the experience of emotions that may arise, physical sensations, and images of the past and present. The role of the thinking mind is to analyze, sum up, and pass judgment on all this as either good or bad based on past experience.

The thinking mind is pretty much on autopilot. It is with our awareness or consciousness that we notice that our thoughts are not still. But the mind does not exist under its own power. It is under the aegis of our consciousness. As our consciousness expands, the think-ing mind also has to be upgraded and trained in new habits of thought based on new information to be gleaned from the present. When the thinking mind wanders, it is consciousness that brings it back to the present and habituates it to the present experience of the body being formed from the invisible Essential Self. This is what transforms the mind—having it be present to ongoing change. This change is constant, as evidenced by the experience of a constant flow of sensations, breathing, and the combustion and transformation of energy and matter throughout the body.

In meditation, we simply experience our thoughts and the im-ages attached to them. We observe them. We accept them. We don't have to agree with them or have them be the evidence of who we are. They are simply the product of the ideas we have had about ourselves up to that point. Each time we meditate with the intention to deepen our connection to our Essential Self, we will deepen our realization of who we are, and emerge as new versions of ourselves.

So, our awareness or consciousness is not centered in the mind—the thinking center of our bodies. So where is it centered then? This is not a question that anyone can answer for us. This is a center that one discovers for oneself. All there is to do is to observe. Observe sensations, observe the space out of which the breath arises, and allow the breath to come up and go out. Observe your emotions as they come and go, allow them to be experienced as a physical phenomenon without labeling anything good or bad.

It is this process of detaching—separating our identity from our thoughts, emotions, sensations, and visualizations—that takes us deeper into a place where we are centered and still. It is the act of detaching from thought, emotion, and sensation that expands our awareness and consciousness. Our consciousness expands and becomes stronger from the simple act of noticing when the mind is "wandering." In meditation, it is this practice of noticing and bringing the mind back to the present moment that takes us deeper into meditation and an expanded awareness of who we are.

It is this process that is called "self-realization." Once we notice our thoughts wandering and bring them back to the present activity, we will begin to locate a new center of our expanding Self.

For this reason, meditation is a practice, a place to discover, play, learn, and become.

So, the mind never really becomes still. What gets still is YOU—as a being that is growing in awareness. As our practice deepens—our awareness of the Self deepens—the thinking mind will be re-oriented around a new set of facts, the reality of on-going change. Soon we will be able to use our minds and not have our minds use us by pulling us into the patterns of the Five Complaints of the Ego. When the mind is stabilized in the present, its single thought becomes one of gratitude and openness to change.

Until that point, the thinking mind will cycle through the Five Complaints of the Ego trying to solve things, wondering why, making things right or wrong, and working its way out of threatening situations. Make room for all of this to be then gently bring it back to the present moment of creation.

The Closing Declaration

With your newly expanded awareness, complete your meditation with the Five Declarations of the Self, which were introduced in Chapter IV.

I can Hear Myself

I Can Feel Myself Changing

I Can See Myself

I Am Connected to ALL Life

I Am Home

Alternatively, at the close of your meditation you can speak the words of your BECOMING. With your newly expanded awareness, begin to notice the vibration of the ESSENCES and DESIRES of your BECOMING. Do this first in the silence and then when you are ready, send this vibration of your BECOMING out of you as an expression of love to everyone around you, including anyone involved in your current circumstances. Silently and inwardly generate the ESSENCE of your BECOMING for everyone because at your personal crossroad you are not alone, all humanity is there with you,

BECOMING. Allow your ESSENCE to radiate to everyone as you make wishes. You can do this by simply and silently saying for example, "May all beings become JOY and COMPASSION."

After Meditation

After your meditation:

- ❖ Begin to notice what is leaving you.
- ❖ Observe what is being pulled in your direction.
- ❖ Allow what's leaving to go.
- ❖ Welcome what's coming in to stay.
- ❖ Do not run after ANYTHING.

Run after nothing and no one. Simply and genuinely invite and make requests then be open to "yes" and "no." Respond to invitations and requests with a simple "no" or "yes." Then do what you said. Don't over-promise or make repeated offers where an offer has been rejected. Be authentic and visible. Move with grace and in peace among others. Do a silent meditation practice for 25 minutes each day. You can start with 5 minutes and increase the length of your meditation each day. I recommend, if you can, that you meditate twice daily, on getting up and before turning in for the night.

GUIDEPOST 19.
BEGIN THIS PRACTICE NOW.
Begin a daily practice of silent meditation. Start

with 10 minutes each morning as soon as you wake up, and 10 minutes each night before going to bed. Gradually you may begin to increase these periods as your attention deepens.

CHAPTER XI

NATURE BASED PRESCRIPTIONS & RITUALS

FOR RESTORING BALANCE

"The best and safest thing is to keep a balance in your life, acknowledge the great powers around us and in us. If you can do that, and live that way, you are really a wise man."

~ EURIPIDES

I N THE LAST CHAPTER, we looked at some of the inner practices that we can employ to gain a new sense of direction and balance when at the crossroads of our lives. We have explored the terrain of our inner world in its purest form in meditation. Also, at the crossroads of our lives we can go to nature to align our inner world with the outer world in as pure a form as we can find. Balance, in its purest form in the outer world, is found in nature. This is the reason a simple walk in the woods refreshes us. Spiritual teacher, Eckhart Tolle, provides a great rationale for this return to nature in his book,

Stillness Speaks.

> *"Whenever you bring your attention to anything natural...you step out of conceptualized thinking, and, to some extent, participate in the state of connectedness with Being in which everything natural still exists... Something of its essence then transmits its essence to you...."*

This "transmission of essence"—the alignment of inner and outer worlds—can help dissolve the wounds that create the dragon-fears encountered at crossroads. But, where in nature can we go and what must we do to heal the specific wounds to which we are vulnerable and slay their attendant dragons? The answer to these questions is offered in the form of what is called a PRESCRIPTION—a recommended course of action that will promote healing. The activity that is to take place in nature as part of this prescription is called a RITUAL.

Nature based PRESCRIPTIONS and RITUALS are powerful keys that we can use to open a gateway into a new experience of ourselves and in so doing find a new direction. They have the ability to bring the elements of our inner nature into alignment with the same elements existing powerfully in their purest forms in nature. This alignment has the ability to help us re-member ourselves in a language without words. It is this "re-membering"—putting ourselves back together—that is the work to be done at the crossroads.

HOW TO DESIGN PRESCRIPTIONS & RITUALS

WE CAN DESIGN SIMPLE PRESCRIPTIONS for ourselves using our KEY ESSENCES and DESIRED ESSENCES. When we identify the element or elements with which our KEY ESSENCES and DESIRED ESSENCES are associated, we can create powerful nature-based prescriptions and rituals for ourselves. These prescriptions can dissolve the fears that unbalance those Essences and that block the unfoldment of our BECOMING.

All of the 25 Essences have elements with which they are associated. The 25 Essences have Primary and Secondary elements with which they are related, with the exception of: SILENCE, UNBOUNDED, PURITY, COMPASSION, and BALANCE. These are each associated with only one of the five elements. These five are called PURE ESSENCES.

The elemental association of each of our KEY and DESIRED ESSENCES suggests the natural physical environment, symbols, and ritual actions to be performed for healing of wounds and the realignment of those Essences within ourselves.

GUIDEPOST 20.
DO THIS NOW

Let's create your prescription and rituals together.

STEP 1: Locate the Primary and Secondary elements associated with the KEY ESSENCES or DESIRED ESSENCES that you want to experience more of or bring into balance. You will find these Essences and their associated Primary and Secondary elements in the Essence Cards in the appendix of this book.

Remember to take each of your KEY or DESIRED ESSENCES one at a time when designing prescriptions and rituals.

For example, if your DESIRED ESSENCE is JOY, the Primary element with which JOY is associated is MINERAL. The Secondary element with which JOY is associated is WATER. (If you begin to think symbolically, you can already see the image of water flowing out of a rock, or of springs and rivers with huge stones. These are some of the places where the essence JOY can be found in nature.)

STEP 2: Identify the Life-Nutrients associated with the Essence. The Primary and Secondary Elements with which JOY, for example, is associated will tell you the Life-Nutrient that you will need to experience more of. As we have seen, JOY is an Essence associated with MINERAL [primary] and WATER [secondary]. Therefore, JOY is a quality that will reconnect you with your authentic VOICE. We know this because MINERAL is the element that empowers our VOICE. Because its secondary element is WATER, JOY also provides an experience of CONNECTION or RECONCILIATION—the energies that bring people together. We know that when those energies are present there is an inner and outer CONNECTION to yourself and others. There is peace and reconciliation, forgiveness and pardoning of the self and others.

Having identified the associated Elements and Life-Nutrients, you are beginning to develop a deeper narrative about the ritual to be performed in nature. We now know that Joy's ritual will involve the symbols of MINERAL and WATER with the intention of restoring VOICE and CONNECTING you with your Self and others through forgiveness and reconciliation.

Here again are the Life-Nutrients provided by each element.

MINERAL	NATURE	FIRE	WATER	EARTH
VOICE – restores our ability to remember/hear our own voice.	HOPE / CHANGE – restores our ability to expand and grow to accommodate changing circumstances.	VISIBILITY / VALUE – allows us to see ourselves clearly –our value, our dreams, and vision for our lives.	CONNECTION – refreshes us and others through forgiveness, peace, and reconciliation.	SAFETY & BELONGING – establishes our ability to rest and be at home in our own bodies and physical environments regardless of the circumstances.

STEP 3: Identify the Life-Areas with which the Primary and Secondary elements of the Essence are associated. Remember,

each Life-Area is a ritual space that honors the Essences associated with it. The Life-Areas with which the Essence is associated tell you where in your life the activity that initiates a deeper experience of that Essence must first be engaged. For example, the Essence JOY has MINERAL as its Primary Essence. MINERAL is associated with the Life-Area, WELL-BEING. The Secondary element of the Essence will also indicate another Life-Area where an activity can be performed. For example, JOY's secondary element is WATER which is associated with FAMILY. So, the activity for JOY is in two Life-Areas: WELL-BEING and FAMILY. This indicates that there may be issues around your personal well-being as well as issues involving members of your family, friends or maybe even one of the difficult people in your life.

Refer to the table below to identify the Life-Areas—the spheres of activity—where the Essences that you are seeking are best honored, activated, and celebrated.

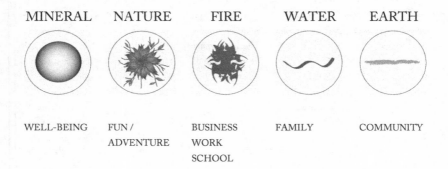

MINERAL	NATURE	FIRE	WATER	EARTH
WELL-BEING	FUN / ADVENTURE	BUSINESS WORK SCHOOL	FAMILY	COMMUNITY

STEP 4: Identify the elemental ACTIVITY with which the Es-

*sence you want to experience is associated. This elemental asso-
ciation will indicate the action you can perform to restore a balanced experience of the Essence you have identified.*

*The table below lists each element and the activities with which
they are associated. Do these actions as part of the nature-based
RITUALS outlined in the next step.*

MINERAL	NATURE	FIRE	WATER	EARTH
Be Silent / Speak Your Truth / Get Busy / Transmit or Acquire new information / Conceal A Secret / Hide/ Wait	Start an initiative / Give Birth / have Intercourse / Move / Risk/ Make Mistakes / Acquire new information/ Roam / Play Music	Display / Unconceal / Dream / Focus / Create something new/ Defend & Hold Space	Act Independently / Forgive/Be compassionate / Simplify / clarify / Be truthful / Flow / Feel / Cry / Let Go / Share & connect with Others - Friends, Family, ancestors	Fellowship / Declare / put things in order / Structure things / Nurture others /Give or Receive /Rest / Get Still/ Get into or close to the ground

*For example, to identify an activity for reconnecting to JOY look
closely at the activities associated with the elements of MIN-
ERAL and WATER. Let your intuition guide you. Allow yourself to feel what action is appropriate for you.*

STEP 5: Locate the places in nature associated with the Essence you want to experience more of. The Primary and Secondary elemental associations of the Essence you are engaging will indicate where in nature you can go to perform your ritual prescription. Remember, your activity will be a symbolic act. Again, let your intuition guide you. A simple intentional activity can be very effective. What is important is that you design it to send a strong symbolic message to yourself that renews your memory of the quality within you that you want to embody more of. Use the table below to help you identify the place in nature where you can perform your activity. The more physical and radical your engagement of nature is, the more powerfully you will experience this realignment. So, in nature, use all your physical senses in your ritual work. Speak, listen, taste, touch, breathe, and look. Be fully present.

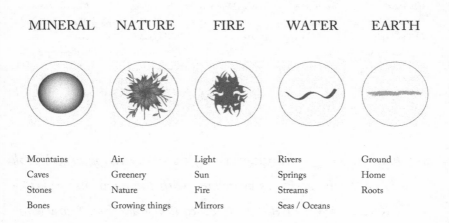

MINERAL	NATURE	FIRE	WATER	EARTH
Mountains	Air	Light	Rivers	Ground
Caves	Greenery	Sun	Springs	Home
Stones	Nature	Fire	Streams	Roots
Bones	Growing things	Mirrors	Seas / Oceans	

As you complete each of the above steps, the outlines of a complete narrative will begin to emerge about the ritual you will choose to perform for the KEY or DESIRED ESSENCE that you want to experience more of, or bring into balance. The narrative indicates the issues to be addressed—alone or with others—the elements to be engaged and the place in nature where you can go to perform your ritual.

When you go into nature to perform your ritual activity first become still. Whether you are alone or with others, as you perform your symbolic actions move within nature with inner stillness powered by your breath. Aim to be "in sync" with the underlying stillness that exists in that location. Inside of that stillness the presence that you experience is the memory of everything that you are.

As a part of your engagement with nature, while you are there you can choose to say one or all of the Five Declarations of the Self. The one that is most powerful should relate to the elemental connection that you are strengthening.

Finally, our relationship with nature is reciprocal. In order to symbolize the quality of that relationship leave something behind as a gift to the ritual space, something that can be absorbed by nature. The simple prescriptions we create can be powerful new narrative bridges that allow for the transmission of nature's essence to refresh and enliven our own fundamental nature.

CHAPTER XII

ALIGNING OUR BODIES WITH NATURE

I N THE END, it all comes down to the body. Our sense of balance is centered in the body. Our body is the meeting point of our inner and outer worlds. Both worlds are linked together by our awareness of that connection. When we are out of touch with our body's energy we become unbalanced. Everything in our awareness—within and without—occurs in the body as a sensation. Every word, thought, emotion, and action emanates from deep sensations in our body. Our bodies and our experiences in them, are printouts of our ideas about who we think we are.

As we have seen, the sense of imbalance results from a focus on the past or a better future, on one or more of the Five Complaints of the Ego, or the wounding emotions of irrelevance, hopelessness, rejection, abandonment, or dislocation. All of these occur as uncomfortable physical sensations in the body. These are the sensations that we try to mask by giving and not keeping our word, by taking on the shadow sides of our KEY ESSENCES, with our addictions, regrets, and dreaming. When these sensations are triggered by circumstances that are out of our control or by difficult people it is easy to use external substances or actions to try to get away from feeling them. We use companionship, food, sex, television, or whatever it takes to stop ourselves from experiencing them.

In this chapter, we will be introduced to an element map of the body that will help us to locate, engage, and move through these difficult sensations—a complex of our dragon-fears, complaints, and limiting ideas about who we are. We will learn new skills to integrate these uncomfortable sensations, and to go deeper into our experience of our essences and open new gateways to our BECOMING.

THE ELEMENT CENTERS OF THE BODY

THERE ARE FIVE ELEMENT CENTERS in our bodies. The energy centers of the five elements are located in specific places of the body. Each center is a channel through which the Essences and Life-Nutrients associated with each element are being channeled as a pure experience that is unique to each of us since it is filtered through:

- ℵ   Our ideas about who we are
- ℵ   Our relationship to the past, present, and future
- ℵ   The quality of our thinking
- ℵ   The emotions on which we are focused
- ℵ   Our physical posture and the way we allow our bodies to move

Each of these filters shapes our inner experience of each Essence and Life-Nutrient and in turn, our experience of the world.

Imagine then that by not allowing ourselves to feel the body's sensations, especially the uncomfortable ones, we are experiencing a reality that is contorted by that avoidance. We must experience these sensations with AWARENESS and ACCEPTANCE if we are to clear these filters and move deeper into our path to BECOMING.

This means being aware of and accepting the sensations of each energy center without trying to change them. Each center will only harden and become darker and denser if its activity is avoided or suppressed. On the other hand, each becomes luminous and translucent with AWARENESS and ACCEPTANCE and is thereby able to shape the beauty of the unique expressions and experiences of the Life-Nutrients and Essences we bring to the world.

Simply, we bloom from the heart of our wounds, our pasts, our thinking: all that we have been and are now fertilizes the new us that is unfolding. AWARENESS and ACCEPTANCE are the keys to our transformation—the expansion of who we know ourselves to be and our experience of life.

The Element Body

To find our center we must first locate it in the body. This means understanding where in the body we are tense, restricting the experience of specific sensations. Below we will locate five focal points that determine our experience of balance in our physical bodies.

The simple element map of the body below will help us to feel and to adjust our inner sense of balance when we are stressed. This adjustment can take the form of simple awareness, a change in posture, a sound, a refocusing of attention, breathing, movement or meditation, among other possibilities.

When we allow ourselves to experience sensations we would otherwise restrict, we become more authentic and available to ourselves and to others.

THE ELEMENT BODY

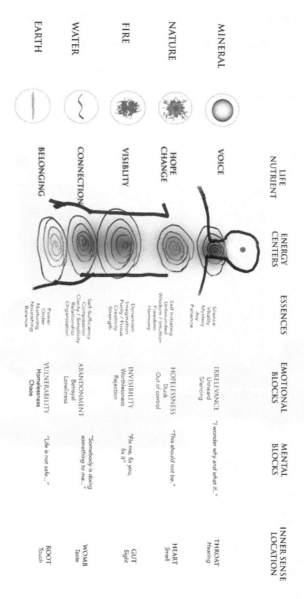

LIFE NUTRIENT		ENERGY CENTERS	ESSENCES	EMOTIONAL BLOCKS	MENTAL BLOCKS	INNER SENSE LOCATION
MINERAL	(symbol)	VOICE	Silence Vitality Mystery Joy Patience	IRRELEVANCE Unheard Silencing	"I wonder why and what if..."	THROAT Hearing
NATURE	(symbol)	HOPE CHANGE	Self Initiating Unbounded Wisdom / Intuition Freedom Harmony	HOPELESSNESS Stuck Out of control	"This should not be."	HEART Smell
FIRE	(symbol)	VISIBILITY	Dynamism Imagination Purity / Focus Creativity Strength	INVISIBILITY Worthlessness Rejection	"Fix me, fix you, fix it"	GUT Sight
WATER	(symbol)	CONNECTION	Self-Sufficiency Compassion Clarity / Simplicity Relationship Organization	ABANDONMENT Betrayal Loneliness	"Somebody is doing something to me..."	WOMB Taste
EARTH	(symbol)	BELONGING	Power Order Nurturing Balance	VULNERABILITY Homelessness Chaos	"Life is not safe..."	ROOT Touch

These centers map the terrain of an inner world that reflects our experience of ourselves. Ultimately, it is this inner experience that is projected outward in the way we identify ourselves, our courage, our self-worth, the ways we relate to others, and how we care for ourselves and the physical spaces we inhabit.

The energy centers of the body are located as follows:

MINERAL

THE THROAT

This center houses the Life-Nutrient of VOICE. Our inner sense of HEARING is located there; not in our physical ears. This is the place where the deepest vibration of our being first manifests as conscious sound. It is in this energy center that this primal vibration of being must be aligned with those vibrations of the self that are eventually heard out loud. This connection is made through the vocal cords located in the throat. So, in some bizarre way our inner ear is in our throats. Our ability to hear is connected to our ability to resist the urge to speak.

All of the Essences associated with Mineral are most deeply felt in the throat. The chief Essence to be felt there is SILENCE—the PURE ESSENCE in Mineral. All the other Essences of Mineral also emanate from there. The throat is a very sensitive area. If we pay attention to the subtle energy in our throats, we may find a whole new world.

The throat center is shut down when we are silenced or unheard, as the flow of the throat's Life-Nutrient is interrupted. The resulting emotion of irrelevance and the sensation of having a "lump in our throat" block the authenticity of our vocal expression.

NATURE

THE HEART

The heart center houses the channel for energies associated with Nature. The Life-Nutrient that feeds our need to experience CHANGE and yet be HOPEFUL is located there. It is in nature that things are circulated, where seasons pass and living things experience the cycle of birth, life, and death. The heart center holds the energy that allows us to be (to exist) in the midst of constant change. This center becomes clogged by our need to control outcomes, by feelings of being stuck and hopeless. Clogged, the heart center affects the free flow of vitality throughout the body.

All of the Essences associated with Nature are most deeply felt in the heart. The chief Essence to be felt there is UNBOUNDEDNESS, the PURE ESSENCE in Nature. Whenever we work with this center, whether through play, vocalizing, breathwork, movement, or yoga, first locate that feeling of UNBOUNDEDNESS, which is also called COURAGE. This is why we hear people say, "Brave heart." All the other Essences of Nature also emanate from there.

The heart center is also where the inner senses of smell are located. It is through this inner sense of smell that we intuit things. That sense of smell is the flow on which information and ideas spring to mind without logic. Hence, people say, "Follow your heart." The heart holds the bits of information that come to us over time to eventually form perfect sentences.

FIRE

THE GUT

The gut center houses the Life-Nutrient VISIBILITY, and channels the Essences associated with FIRE. This energy center is located at the center of the stomach, right below the diaphragm.

All of the Essences associated with FIRE are most deeply felt in the gut. Chief among them is PURITY, sometimes called Focus—the PURE ESENCE of FIRE.

Our inner sense of SIGHT is also located in the gut. To witness the world unfold like a movie, we must open our inner eye in the gut. We see the unseen with our gut. To really see someone or to know the truth about a situation we may have to see with physical eyes, but we must also plug into the energy in our guts. We have to make sure this energy is flowing freely and is not blocked by our own fears of INVISIBILITY, REJECTION, and WORTHLESSNESS. The gut is the place where we truly see ourselves and the world.

WATER

THE WOMB

The WOMB center houses the streams of energy that connect us to each other. In men and women, it's located just below the navel. We all came by way of the WOMB. It is a commonality through which we are all connected, making WOMB energy very powerful. Regardless of gender we carry this connective and reproductive life force in this area of our bodies. The Life-Nutrient CONNECTION is channeled there. The womb is the energy center associated with WATER. The purest Essence to be found there is RELATIONSHIP.

Disconnection of this commonality is evidenced when we say things like, "He is wrong and I am right." These are words of separation. Wounds of abandonment and betrayal obscure the flow of energy in this center, restricting our ability to honor our deep connections to one another.

EARTH

THE ROOT

This energy center houses the Life-Nutrient that gives us a sense of BELONGING & HOME, as well as all of the Essences associated with EARTH. The ROOT center is located in the area at the base of the spine. The purest Essence to be felt there is BALANCE. Our greatest sense of BALANCE is experienced and expressed through this channel, which can be obscured if we feel dislocated, homeless, chaotic, or unsafe. We are susceptible to overdoing the Essences associated with this center: We overdo NURTURING & NOURISHING to give ourselves a sense of HOME; we overdo ORDER & BALANCE, becoming stubborn and set in our ways, to ensure continuity.

The ROOT is also where the Essence of POWER is located. When we are wounded there, this gives rise to hoarding, greed, and the accumulation of the trappings of externalized power.

THE ANSWERS ARE WITHIN YOU

WHEN ATTEMPTING TO RESTORE BALANCE, the basic questions we tend to ask are: Why? How? Who? Where? When? The answers to these questions first come as a vibration, a tone produced in the being of our true nature. It is this tone, when all of the centers are aligned, that creates a magnetic field that attracts the information, people, resources, and experiences that are its equivalent. The production of breath is how each energy center in our body vitalizes itself. Each center is actually alive—inhaling and exhaling. All parts of our bodies are breathing. Each inhalation pulls through the Life-Nutrient that is that energy center's externalized equal. Each exhalation transmits from an inner invisible source, the Life-Nutrient associated with that center. It is the complete meeting of these internal and external energies that opens each center and has us being more alive and balanced. As we become still and allow this meeting to take place in each energy center, this tone will become stronger.

Below is an inner practice that will help us to realign the vibration of each of the elemental energy centers in our bodies.

GUIDEPOST 21.
DO THIS NOW
THE BLOOM MEDITATION

This exercise can be done as a silent sitting, walking, or moving meditation.

Bring your awareness to the place just between your eyebrows. Think of this area as your "pointer." Feel the subtle sensations or the movement of activity there. Throughout this meditation, you will keep your awareness of this activity while also being aware of activity in other energy centers of your body.

THE THROAT

Start with the energy center at the back of your throat. Bring your awareness to this center. Be aware that the activity there seeks to connect you with your authentic VOICE. The sensations you are experiencing there are your unfolding VOICE. Know that the Essences housed there are deep SILENCE, VITALITY, MYSTERY/THE UNKNOWN (which can feel like the "lump in the throat" that we get when we don't know what to say or do), JOY (the house of laughter), and IMMORTALITY/PATIENCE (our sense of timelessness). Tilt your head back and expose your throat. Become aware of the vulnerability of having that area open. Keep your head up and the area exposed. Feel for any sensations of discomfort. Don't try to change them. Allow them to "be" with the awareness that the activity you are experiencing is part of the unfolding of the energy behind your authentic VOICE. These sensations of vulnerability are what shape your humanity and allow you to be heard as a fellow traveler, with a unique experience and tone. Imagine that this center has a life of its own and that every cell and atom there is breathing. Imagine that you are holding an egg in the back of your throat. Drop your jaw, lower the back of your tongue, and allow your throat center to breathe itself. Allow it to release and pull into itself the external energy that will vitalize it. Let's do the same for each of the other four centers.

THE HEART

Keeping your awareness on the field between your eyebrows, bring your attention to the energy center in the middle of the chest just below the collar bones. Keeping your throat open, consciously drop your shoulders and slightly raise your chest allowing the heart area to be exposed and vulnerable. Feel for any discomfort. When you find the place where you feel the area is most exposed and vulnerable, hold there and allow the area to breathe. Feel the breath entering and leaving the area. This area is most easily blocked by hopelessness. The activity that is unfolding there is your ability to be essentially unchanged in any circumstance. We call this HOPE. Know that the Essence of BOUNDLESSNESS is located at the center of this area. BOUNDLESSNESS is surrounded by SELF-INITIATION (the activity that causes new growth), *WISDOM/INTUITION (the energy that allows you to know things without logic), FREEDOM and HARMONY.* Feel the activity of this area. Don't try to get comfortable. Search for the uncomfortable spaces there and make peace with them. Allow those uncomfortable spaces to breathe by allowing the breath to enter and leave the area.

THE GUT

When you are ready, while keeping awareness of your pointer, move on. Place your attention on the energy center located in the gut. The center of this area is right below the middle of your rib cage, at the center of your diaphragm. Open the center by adjusting your body as needed. Make the area open and vulnerable. Try to imagine that were someone to punch you there you would really feel it. Open it up. Allow the area to breathe. Feel for its vulnerability. The gut is an area where we feel rejection and shame most powerfully. These are the emotions that block this center. Be aware that this center, when open, houses your ability to *SEE.* This is where the Life-Nutrient *VISIBILITY* is housed. Know that when the gut center is open you can see things clearly. Allow the area to breathe. Dynamism, imagination, focus/*PURITY, CREATIVITY,* and *STRENGTH* are most powerfully felt in this area. Know that at the center of this field is the Essence *PURITY.* Begin to feel for the center and, by allowing it to breath in and out, feel the vibration being released as the pure energy of *FIRE.* Stay there as long as you need to. Make space for discomfort. Any discomfort there are scars from rejection and shame felt when you were not yet conscious.

THE WOMB

When you are ready, using the pointer between your eyes, become aware of your womb center. It is the area directly below your navel. Men, yes, you have a womb. Adjust your body and breathing to feel the activity of this center. It is a center that can be elusive, especially for men, so be persistent in allowing yourself to be aware of it and permit it to breathe. Notice the breath being pulled into and departing the area and its activity. Deliberately for a few breaths expand and contract the area with your breathing to wake yourself up to it. Again, feel for the areas of discomfort and allow those areas to breathe. The Life-Nutrient in this area is CONNECTEDNESS. This area is the womb; everyone passes through a womb to come into this life. The centering Essence, the one most deeply felt there is RELATIONSHIP. The womb is surrounded by COMPASSION and self-sufficiency, organization/FLOW), and clarity/SIMPLIC-ITY. It is a center that can be shut down by feelings of betrayal and abandonment. Any discomfort there may be remnants of these traumas. Allow the area to breathe. Imagine that you are coming through these wounded places and shaping your own unique ability to relate authentically, profoundly, and compassionately to others.

THE ROOT

When you are ready, use your pointer to become aware of the root energy center. It is lowest area of the pelvis, the place that you sit on, that points directly to the earth. Adjust your body if necessary. Move slightly. Use your breath to expand the area. Pull up using your "bathroom" muscles to become aware of the activity of the area. Feel for the energetic center of it. Right there, pointing downward toward the earth is the Essence BALANCE. Around it you will find the Essences nourishing, nurturing, order, and power. This is where the Life-Nutrient HOME/BELONGING is housed. The activity of the energy here can be very subtle. In the course of everyday life, you can easily become disconnected from it by chaos and physical movement. You may be wounded by the trauma of sudden dislocation, violence, or a feeling that you don't belong. It is an area that can mask great pain. Again, allow yourself to feel for the place in this part of your body where you are most uncomfortable and vulnerable. Allow these uncomfortable places to breathe. Imagine that the breath is being called into you from this area to catalyze your power, to bring order to your world, to cause you to nurture and nourish yourself and your world, and to maintain an experience of balance.

After you have brought your awareness to each area, feel free to return to each as needed.

With your newly expanded awareness, complete your practice with the Five Declarations of the Self, which were introduced in Chapter IV.

I can Hear Myself

I Can Feel Myself Changing

I Can See Myself

I Am Connected To All Life

I Am Home

After your practice:

- ❖ Begin to notice what is leaving you.
- ❖ Observe what is being pulled in your direction.
- ❖ Allow what's leaving to go.
- ❖ Welcome what's coming in to stay.
- ❖ Do not run after ANYTHING.

Run after nothing and no one. Simply and genuinely invite and make requests then be open to "yes" and "no." Respond to invitations and requests with a simple "no" or "yes." Then do what you said. Don't over-promise or make offers where there is no request. Be authentic and visible. Move with grace and in peace among others.

Epilogue

FOURS YEAR LATER, the book was complete. Yes, it took that long. There were more moments of self-doubt and journeying deeper inside myself in order to connect to life's nutrients. I faced formidable warriors, found my cheerleaders and a midwife, and built a community.

In so many ways I have learnt that to balance it all, I simply have to become <u>my</u> all.

In writing I have taken new ground for myself.

In the end, I knew it was complete because through the process of its birthing I began to experience myself more completely. I am learning to embrace my shadows and to be more compassionate with my humanity. I learnt to honor my community and to write for their ears and needs. Above all else, I feel more at home in the world as I am.

In the midst of the journey, an email arrived one morning in my inbox unexpectedly. It was a letter from Madra. Here is what she wrote.

> *Dear Olu*
>
> *I'm writing you from my veranda -- which is a corner of my apartment with all windows full of different plants, all in various stages. I have a chaise here where*

*I can sit and do my staring-out-the-window medita-
tion. I love this spot. I've watched a lot of mornings
come in through these windows. I find myself looking
forward to coming home and just sitting here to look
at my plants and stare out the window.*

*I'm writing to thank you for guidance and allowing me
to Journey with you. You have helped me to do, un-do,
and not do a lot of things I could name.*

*This has been the best year of my life -- the most con-
scious and the most abundant. I've done concrete
things -- some of which you have seen posted to Facebook! I paid off a big debt. I don't care about buying
random consumer cuteness anymore. I spend my
money on structure. Things that simplify - like buying
fresh flowers. There are all these tangible and intangi-
ble things I do now that I didn't do before that are for
me and that would have seemed inaccessible before.*

*There is a lot of roaring in my ears or there was a con-
stant pressure brought on by many things in my life
and the absence of many things from my life. That
roaring seems quiet more often now. I don't know that
it goes away because I think that is part of life, at least
my life. I don't want to be stress-free. I want to have
some retreat space to just maintain myself -- as Gwen-
dolyn Brooks put it: conduct your blooming in the
whip and noise of the whirlwind.*

My ultimate desire could be having a voice, making

things happen, being unbounded... my professional de-
sire is power and influence but professional being isn't
all I want. I'm on a path to finding or feeling some core
desires or maybe just on a path to finding a path
through each moment. I'm scaling back a bit. The way
that I'm sitting here on my veranda writing this letter
is where I'm at and that's what I want right now - to
be where I am.

You advised me to approach setting up my new place
as a series of installations. Actually -- that is a remix of
what you said! But I applied what you said to the task
at hand, which was setting up a new home. The ve-
randa is one spot. My window in my room is really
beautiful -- I have an orchid there that I thought was
over and it actually has three new stems and I think it's
going to flower, but I'm not sure. I'm watching it with
a lot of anticipation!!! There are seashells from when I
went to Florida after completing my project in May --
the first time I ever rewarded myself for a job well-
fucking-done.

Anyway abundance.

I thought simplicity and clarity would mean less, cut-
ting things out because those words directed me to
clear the clutter but actually I feel that my life is fuller
now. Abundant.

I am the only one who can make myself at home. I can
just sit in a chair wherever I am and go to this place for

a second, 20 minutes, an hour, however long. I now know meditation. This whole process has been transformative. I tend to force things and to be rigid especially under stress. So, when it comes up, I let it be and pass on.

Everything is different now to where I was this time last year and where I was when I opted to sign up for your coaching. I think I got to ask the questions I truly needed to ask myself in order to move forward but I wouldn't have known the words or the structure to put them into.

Right now, it's about movement and being myself. I can look around this apartment and say: "Yeah, this is me." This isn't from a catalog. This isn't for the neighbors you know how that goes. I eat for myself.

I'm so much nicer now than I would have been a year ago. Less agitated. Less craven, compulsive, and impulsive.

Your process helped me to find some quiet apart from that noise and pressure and I'm so much more here for it.

To be earnest and not naive and obsessive. To be dedicated and not compulsive. To be giving and not a martyr. And so on. A sort of non-doing. I don't have to strive anymore. I can just be however and whoever I am and that is the journey. "Be" is just two letters and

seems so simple but I'm appreciating now how com-
plicated and exciting that is, day-to-day moment-to-
moment. I can't theorize it. I guess it's a kind of prac-
tice. But I see that I am approaching more things in
my life in ways that are, I guess you could say, health-
ier.

Thank you so much for making yourself available to
your own path and letting me walk part of the way. I
didn't want the year to end without letting you know I
found a path to myself through the journaling and
challenges and instructions that you offered. While I'm
not really there yet, I look around and my surroundings
vibe with me. A lot of what I'm going to do today
comes from these veranda moments.

Thank you so much for helping me.

Madra

APPENDIX

THE ESSENCE CARDS

The Essence Cards™ are made up 25 cards that represent a complete palate of the 25 dimensions of the human personality as observed through the lens of the five elements of MINERAL, NATURE, FIRE, WATER, and EARTH and their attributes. These cards describe their "light" and "dark" sides, what sets them off, what balances them, and what is possible when they evolve together. Each card describes an archetypical human personality, each with unique attitudes, perceptions, thoughts, emotional triggers, and responses that express "in balance" and "out of balance."

You will gain insights from recognizing yourself—who you now are and what you want to become—in specific cards, the archetypes they represent and combinations thereof. When working with these cards you will select cards as answers to simple questions. By bringing this information to the level of conscious thought, you will be stimulated to consider change and growth. This recognition can be life transforming, pointing to the shifts needed to accomplish difficult projects, resolve conflicts, and experience a new sense of inner balance and direction.

HOW THEY WERE CREATED

The Essence Cards™ are the result of a series of insights. **The first insight** comes from the world view of the Dagara people of West

Africa, in whose cosmology the five elements of mineral, nature, fire, water, and EARTH account for the creation and balance of the cosmos. This truth is echoed by Vedic Rishis—the wise men of India who declared:

Out of Brahma, [which is the Higher Self] came space; out of space came air; out of air, fire; out of fire, water; out of water, earth; out of earth… the body of all humanity.

TAITTRIYA UPANISHAD

Though the words used were different, the energies to which both cultures speak are the same. Mineral and Space are the same element, as both are symbols for an energy found within the core of the hardest substances known to man, yet ethereal enough to be known as Space. Similarly, Nature and Air point to the same element, because all that the Dagara knew as nature – the plants and animals – breathed air.

What did these two seemingly distant cultures know that had them utter the same truth? They knew the same truths that are reflected in the cultural and spiritual traditions of the people of ancient Egypt, the Yoruba of West Africa, and the Asiatic peoples. What they knew was a simple truth that Love, the essence of life, expresses as these elements, and that the well-being of human beings and the planet rests on the inner and outer balance of these five elements.

The second insight came when Indian seers again peered deeply into the void beyond time and space and provided us a profound snapshot of Love in the form of 25 qualities. In our time,

Deepak Chopra has popularized them as "the qualities of pure consciousness" in his book *Creating Affluence.* There he credited them to Maharishi Mesh Yogi—the founder of Transcendental Meditation, as Meshi Yogi's codification of the qualities of the unified field out of which everything springs.

I call these 25 qualities the "Essences of Love." They are the pure stuff that creates the Universe. I believe that what these seers described are the same qualities articulated by the Apostle Paul in his letter to the early Christian church at Corinth and the same energies embodied by the Orishas of the Yoruba tradition of West Africa, amongst others. What they saw are the qualitative ways in which Love, the power that creates the Universe, is expressed.

The third insight dawned over time and brought the first two together. It was the realization that these 25 Essences also describe the five elements of which the peoples of the world have consistently spoken.

The final insight followed from the first three. If Love is the source of all things, it follows that these elements and essences are the make-up of human beings and provide information about our very nature.

I have come to understand that Love expresses itself in human beings as 25 distinct personality types or behavioral patterns that mirror the 25 essences and the five elements. The behavioral patterns that dominate our lives reflect the unique elemental make-up of each human being, in balance and out of balance.

I believe that the essences in us are seeking to evolve, to be expressed through and as us. When they get stuck and don't evolve, we experience ourselves as "stressed," being "out of balance," going around in circles, forgetting our life's vision and purpose. When they do evolve, they balance and transform the experiences of our lives, causing us to see clearly our life's vision, take balanced action, and create peaceful communities. But these essences can only evolve with our conscious awareness, permission, and attention. When we are unconscious of this desire and do not give the essences our attention, they express in unbalanced ways. When we give this process our attention, we engage actively in the evolution of our character and as a result, deepen our range of choices about what we can experience and accomplish.

The Essence Cards are born from these insights.

THE PLAY OF ESSENCES

Key Essences & Desired Essences

ALL THE ESSENCES are in us at various stages of manifestation. These cards provide us with a way to consciously participate - as co-creators - in the evolution of our experience and the world.

At any given time, most of us can identify with at least three of these 25 qualities and would describe them as our best qualities. These are often qualities we summoned to help us survive challenging times when we were children—when we were silenced, felt hopeless, invisible, abandoned, or dislocated. As we grow older, we rely on these strengths during similarly difficult times. Eventually, they become the way we currently experience ourselves for better or for worse. These qualities are called our KEY ESSENCES.

There are three qualities, on the other hand, which are called our DESIRED ESSENCES. These are qualities of which we do not seem to have a conscious experience, yet consistently wish we did. Were we to be asked to name our KEY and DESIRED ESSENCES a year from now, there would most likely be changes since our essences are in a constant state of flux as our conscious awareness of ourselves expands and deepens.

Our KEY ESSENCES tend to become out of balance and express as their shadow sides when we are stressed—triggered by the circumstances to which we are vulnerable. Similarly, our DESIRED ESSENCES, the qualities we want to experience more of, can express in our behaviors in an unbalanced way when we summon them as a response to stressful situations. For example, when FOCUS is summoned and used to get a job done, but also burns everyone and everything else in its path. These conditions of imbalance occur when we are challenged to feel difficult emotions—to be real with ourselves in ways to which we are not accustomed; when we encounter challenging PROJECTS and face WARRIORS—difficult people who push our buttons. These shadows become our MASKS—inauthentic ways of coping.

The 25 personality archetypes described in the cards map not only the archetypes of individuals, but also of whole countries, communities, and organizations. The activity of the shadow sides of these archetypes underpin the conflicts between individuals as well as nations, or any group with a shared identity. These shadows also hobble the productivity and innovation of individuals as well as organizations and communities.

When we express our shadow sides we are not present—not living in the moment with gratitude for the resources we have and acceptance of ourselves. Knowing the MASKS we wear is among the first steps towards self-discovery, true innovation, and personal and planetary transformation.

Becoming

Our KEY ESSENCES want to evolve and merge with our DESIRED ESSENCES to catalyze and deepen our evolution, allowing us to make quantum leaps in our experience of life. This process is called BECOMING. The gift of the WARRIOR or of a challenging PROJECT is our BECOMING. The energies of WARRIORS and difficult PROJECTS are not personal; they are life's way of having us *experience* our BECOMING. The choice to BECOME is often coupled with a choice to accept difficult emotions and facts. When we do not BECOME, we seemingly have the same things happen over and over again with similar results. This costs us well-being, personal productivity, effectiveness, personal satisfaction, and relationships. The choice to BECOME is the choice to expand the way we know ourselves so we can hold and *experience* more of life.

The goal of our life's journey—the Essential Journey—is our BECOMING. Knowing our BECOMING, being able to declare it, feel and allow it, provides a high platform from which we can see new VISIONS for our lives and for the world. When we make our gifts serve our VISION and seek to give our gifts away to everyone, we have found our life's purpose.

Your ESSENCES Are Your True Voice

Everything is vibration. All physical matter is sound expressing at various frequencies—levels of conscious awareness. Physical matter is the VOICE of creation experienced at various frequencies. Everything is being spoken into existence. Your unique voice creates your experience of yourself and your world. Your *true* VOICE is the combination of the ESSENCES you have allowed yourself to experience with conscious awareness. Your true voice is what the people of ancient Egypt called your HEKA—the unique vibration your Soul emits as it journeys. Your VOICE is the vibration of the ESSENCES that you have embodied. We each carry a unique voice and it is immediately creative—creating each cell and organ of our bodies, our minds, and our experience of life itself.

PRIMARY & SECONDARY ESSENCES

BEFORE YOU START TO USE THE CARDS, here is what you need to know about the element make-up of each Essence. Each Essence has a Primary element with which it is associated. This is the element that best describes the Essence's most dominant features. For example, the Essence NURTURING is primarily associated with the element EARTH. Each Essence also has a Secondary element with which it is associated, such that NURTURING is also associated with the element of FIRE. The exceptions to this rule are Silence, Unbounded, Purity, Relationship, and Balance, which are PURE ESSENCES and as such are associated with, or best described by, only one element.

In the chart below Primary elements appear at the top of each column, while Secondary elements are indicated by the symbol for each element that appears at the start of each row of Essences. Each Essence, with the exception of the PURE ESSENCES, has a TWIN ESSENCE. TWIN ESSENCES are Essences that embody the same two elements. For example, WISDOM and IMAGINA-TION are TWIN ESSENCES because each is related to the elements FIRE and NATURE.

In an attempt to name what is experienced, multiple adjectives are used to describe the attributes of each ESSENCE on the cards. Each adjective can be used interchangeably. Use the name that is most resonant for you. For example, PURITY is also called FOCUS; CLARITY is also called SIMPLICITY, etc.

	MINERAL	NATURE	FIRE	WATER	EARTH
	Silence	Self-Initiating	Dynamism	Self-Sufficiency	Power
	Vitality	Unbounded	Imagination	Compassion	Order
	Mystery	Wisdom	Purity	Simplicity	Nurturing
	Joy	Freedom	Creativity	Relationship	Nourishing
	Patience	Harmony	Strength	Organization	Balance

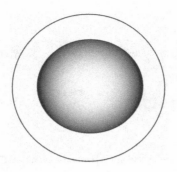

SILENCE
Open · Quiet · Observer

Deep Listening

Mineral | Mineral

Pure Essence of MINERAL

You are a cool, quiet observer; a deep listener. You seem to sit still, off to the side of things. You have a long memory and an ability to discern the motives of others.

Like a stone, you can sit still and take everything in. You are a quiet, understated observer; a deep listener who seems to be beyond the fray, off to the side of things. You appear not to be paying close attention, but you seldom miss much. Secretly you transmit everything. Others look to your every move for indications of what to do next. You have a long memory and a keen ability to discern the stories and motives of others. You are relied on for your knowledge and clear-eyed acceptance. In a group, you tend to carry great weight, though not always as the leader. You are the true indicator of the state of things. You are here to help people remember their gifts and purpose. When silence is balanced, it can hear not just others, but also itself—your own inner voices, emotions, intentions, and desires. Silence can observe the world as a reflection of its own inner state. People who consciously choose this quality are the ears of the Creator. This power is best harvested in very high, remote places or in places naturally sealed from sound—mountains/ hilltops, elevated natural structures.

Shadow
The Hang Man

Feeling unheard or misunderstood triggers your shadow. This brings on self-doubt and a generalized sense of confusion. When stressed in this way, you tend to give people and situations that offend you by not listening or misunderstanding, a lot of rope so they can hang themselves. In other words, you will let people do what they want to do with the full knowledge that they will fall flat on their faces. When you are attacked, you can become a harsh, though silent, judge of other people's actions. To avoid feeling misunderstood you will set yourself further and further apart from others. You do not like heated conversations. When this happens, you tend not to share what is on your mind; this is how you protect yourself. You will seem to be working with others, but behind the scenes you can be seen causing disruption. Others will accuse you of being silently manipulative. You are good at giving the "silent treatment." You may be called cynical, malicious, or arrogant. When you have to enter the fray and deal with others, you can appear isolated, distant, and aloof. People tend not to know what's going on with you. If you feel unheard, you will react by speaking in parables and giving hints under your breath. Later you will speak your truth firmly and see what people do with it. In extreme circumstances when you feel unheard [and you would have to be highly upset for this to happen], like a long dormant volcano, you can erupt suddenly and loudly. Your last words are usually, "I told you so."

VITALITY
AWARE · CURIOUS · ENGAGED

Life Activated

MINERAL | NATURE

Twin Essence ~ SELF-INITIATING

You are conduit for information and experience. Always on the hunt for what is important; you are engaged with the people and things around you. You are a constant fount of energy and information. Even when still, you are on the move.

A firm believer that information changes things, you share information that makes a difference. People rely on you to get the word out and to keep them connected with news about others. You are relied upon for your liveliness, to make introductions, and to jumpstart difficult conversations. It takes energy for others to keep up with you, as you think, speak, and move quickly and with purpose. You can get people to talk about anything; to give information about themselves that they would not otherwise provide. In a team, you work well with people and are not afraid to take the initiative. You have the ability to sort through all sorts of information and find what is vital and useful. The information you share is important, relevant, and timely. Your intention is to be a conduit of vital information and hope.

Shadow
Busy Body

Your shadow is triggered when you are made to feel silenced, irrelevant, hopeless, and stuck. When you feel this way, you can be excessively talkative and nosy. On the other hand, when ignored you will withhold vital information. To ensure that your voice is heard you will say whatever comes to your mind though this can be off-putting to the people around you. To avoid feeling stagnant you will always be on the move. People may say that you are "fast." For you, to stop moving is to die. This is how you keep yourself alive. To others you appear to be always busy, always on the run. You are in and out of everything and everyone's business. You will often complain of feeling tired, but this only spurs you on; tired and hopeless is not what you want to feel. People complain that they never seem to have your full attention; you can talk, but do not seem to listen carefully. You will cut people off because they are not getting to the point quickly enough. Though your energy is relentless, when things appear to be truly lost you will take to your bed, saying you are "burnt out." When you have concluded that you are really not being heard you will go silent, hoarding and dispensing vital information until you are romanced back to relevance. Famous first words: "What's going on?

Well, if you had asked me I would have told you."

MYSTERY

Invisible · Private · Un-manifest

Unknown & Unknowable

Mineral | Fire

Twin Essence ~ DYNAMISM

You are very comfortable with the unknown and un-knowable. You step into situations very easily and sort things out when they happen. You have a very different take on what is "real."

Like a mystic sitting alone in a cave, you are very comfortable with the unknown and unknowable. Your work is to inquire into life's riddles and to solve them in a way that opens up a new world for everyone. You have most likely seen things or had deep experiences that others have not. As a result, you step into challenging situations easily because you have a very different take on what is "real." People are drawn to you because you seem to know secrets, things that others do not. In a team, you are the memory of the group, you will always remind the group about what they are forgetting.

Shadow
The Invisible One

Your shadow is triggered when you feel over-exposed, misunderstood, underestimated, or like a fraud. Sometimes you take on too much risk. You can go into hiding and disappear completely or hide in plain sight. When you feel you have to prove or justify yourself you tend to publicly take on too much risk and can go too far. You do this in order to avoid feeling like a con artist or a fraud. When you go too far you are seen by others as crazy because you will not see things that were obvious to others from the start. People sometimes think you are reckless and blame you for taking them into uncharted territory. You have difficulty answering the question "How?" You will simply claim that you are "misunderstood." You do not like being exposed or so you say. You do not like being underestimated or publicly challenged about what you can or cannot do. Under pressure, you tend to hide your head in the sand and stick to your course of action instead of facing what others say are the facts. As this plays itself out, buoyed by your Twin Essence, DYNAMISM, you become the center of the attention you said you did not want. Your famous last words: "I believe. I remember when…"

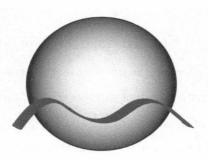

JOY
CONTENT · FULFILLED · EASYGOING

The Fount of Laughter

MINERAL | WATER

Twin Essence ~ SELF-SUFFICIENCY

Contentment is your middle name. You can fit in easily. You are a genuine source of happiness and gratitude. Naturally at ease, you can find laughter in most situations.

Like a spring that bursts forth from a rock, you are a source of genuine happiness and refreshment. You carry with you a genuine feeling of gratitude and joyfulness. You love company and feelings of fullness and contentment. You are naturally easygoing and can find humor in most situations. You have a gift for causing laughter so people love to be around you. You are the life of the party. Without you around things tend to get too serious. With you the party never stops. More so than others you will do whatever it takes to feel good, make a connection with others, and be happy. You are always seen to be making a good joke, providing comic relief when things are stressful. Somehow you find all this joy within yourself. You have the ability to connect people of different backgrounds through their shared humanity and experience of the simple things in life.

Shadow
Bum

Your shadow is triggered when you feel silenced and abandoned. You tend to avoid conflict of ANY kind. You will avoid anything that will stop the party and the laughter for too long. This is how you avoid feeling alone; it's how you keep feeling connected. The avoidance of conflict could include resistance to working with people or in situations that are too demanding. People may accuse you of being a bum, lazy, or too "happy-go-lucky." You tend not to defend yourself if attacked. When you are attacked, you will humor your attacker. You will try not to let your hurt feelings show. Often you are described as a "cool" person, but underneath you are angry with people who attack your character and say mean things about you. Everything is always great with you or so you say. Because you seldom complain, your needs often go unmet. When you do speak up and tell it like it is, people tend not to take you too seriously. However, you do not stay unhappy for long. Your famous last words: "Don't worry; be happy."

PATIENCE
PERMANENT · STILL · IMMORTAL

The Pace of Life

MINERAL | EARTH

Twin Essence ~ POWER

You can see the long view and you are aware of the past. Because you have a great sense of the pace of life, you can wait for things to happen.

Like an aged rock, you feel like you have been around for a long time. You see the long view and are aware of the past. You can wait for things to happen. You have a great sense of the pace of life. While others around you seem ruffled, you are well grounded. You don't mind taking it slow to preserve the sense of community and continuity. Others depend on you to keep things steady, to keep a cool head, and provide an anchor when the going gets rough. People think of you as being grounded. You have a reputation of being "sure footed." Aided by your Twin Essence, POWER, you are able to take the high road, see the long-term implications of things, and devise the best strategy to marshal the necessary resources.

Shadow
Procrastinator

You do not like to feel overwhelmed, chaotic, or panicked by the restrictions of time. When you feel that you have to make a decision that may upset the balance of things, you are paralyzed by self-doubt. To avoid feeling panicked and in order to feel in control, you would rather not do anything or say anything. When you feel under pressure to act to defend yourself, you tend to become stuck or flat-footed. You will tend not to share information or present your point of view until you think you know what you are doing. People will accuse you of procrastination or of not following up, of being asleep on the job. They will not bring things to you for your input or decision for fear that you will take forever or not get back to them. In this way, you are often excluded or not kept in the loop. Moving slowly is how you seem to get back at people and situations that are insisting that you act now. This tends to go on with you forever. Your famous last words: "Let's all keep a cool head"

SELF-INITIATING
SELF-STARTER • RESPONSIBLE

The First Response

MINERAL | MINERAL

Twin Essence ~ VITALITY

You do not need to be jump-started. You are able to respond to things without being led, yet move with great confidence. To you most things are familiar and move only when you move.

You are always the first to take action. You do not need to be jumpstarted. A natural leader, you are able to respond to things without being led. You are committed to shattering the status quo. You are not committed to "business as usual." More so than most, you have come to terms with the good things about yourself as well as the things that are not so nice. You are very much grounded in the present moment so you are seldom hobbled by a great deal of self-doubt. This allows you to exhibit true self-confidence. You are about solutions, not rehashing problems. Your aim is to see how far you can take things. You can articulate your reasons clearly. The people around you rely on you to take the initiative when things need to be done. They know they can count on you to deliver what you promised. You are not much concerned with answering the question "How?" You seem to be able to think on your feet. You seem to always have something to say or are able to take action that puts you in control, rather than at the mercy of circumstances. You seem not to spend a lot of time complaining about what's not being done, or what is being done to you. You will take on a task and follow it through to completion. You have the tireless energy that is provided to you by your Twin Essence, VITALITY. With this energy, you are able to act in a way that invigorates and motivates people around you. You are comfortable being the first and wonder why others aren't.

Shadow
The Upstart

You cannot tolerate anything that signals a roadblock. This shadow is triggered by feelings of being stuck, powerless, out of control, or misunderstood. In order to feel in control and take charge of things, you will often take actions and articulate your point of view in a way that does not consider the emotions of the people around you. Others mistake your actions as being purely self-centered or arrogant, but they are actually driven by this need to control things, set things in motion, and to be heard. When you are accused in this way or are feeling out of touch, you tell people that you lack knowledge or information about what is going on. You will frequently check in with others to make sure you are making the right decision or are under-standing the situation correctly. Usually others will tell you that you were right to do what you did. This justification fuels your impulse to act on your own even when you are uncertain. As a result, you tend to lose touch with your peers who have less tolerance for risk or who want to act more communally/conventionally. They may feel alien-ated. Your actions can cost you their genuine love and affinity. In extreme cases, you can become totally incapacitated by self-doubt and procrastination and unable to commit. This tends to happen when you have taken on way too much responsibility and are in over your head. When this happens, your natural VITALITY deserts you and instead of looking forward to engaging others, you want to drop everything and run away. Famous last words: "Please keep up!"

UNBOUNDED
LIMITLESS · WILD · UNSTOPPABLE

The Record Breaker

NATURE | NATURE

Pure Essence of NATURE

A shape-shifter, you can adapt to any environment. You do not see barriers and can magically appear on the other side of a divide. You will not stop where other people do. You will adapt and grow from wherever you are.

You are like the wind: you are unstoppable and do not see barriers. You do not stop where other people do. You see the world as a huge place and can make yourself at home wherever you are. You want to touch and experience everything. You are a huge personality that fills a room. You are unselfconscious, accepting of yourself, and your uniqueness. You honor what is being expressed through you in the moment, with little attention to the status quo. You live very much in the present moment and respond to that moment. Even if a place is not your home you will make it so. People love to have you in their home or presence because you expand every space you enter, bringing it new life. You are committed to being free to see and experience everything and to breaking down barriers to make the world a larger space for everyone.

Shadow
The Outlaw

This shadow is triggered when you are feeling restricted, controlled, or out of control. You do not like activities or environments that are too structured. You do not like feeling hemmed in. When you feel restricted your identity as a maverick is seriously threatened. In response, you will act out by violating boundaries secretly or publicly. You will rebel. For example, you may steal things, say anything to anyone, enter taboo relationships, or just do anything to flout public opinion and establish yourself on the other side of a boundary. You do not know where to stop. You are seen as a bit of an outlaw or vagabond. Sometimes you wonder if secretly some good friends of yours may not now be avoiding you in certain circumstances. People wonder about you because they never know what you are going to do or what is going to come out of your mouth. Often you fear that you will not find your way back home…that you have gone too far. When this happens, you revert to the polar opposite of your nature. You impose restrictions on yourself to manage your behavior. You will go into retreat and withdraw from friends and family only to reappear later chastened, if only for the moment.

WISDOM
INTUITIVE · KNOWING · MAGICAL

Pure Knowledge

NATURE | FIRE

Twin Essence ~ IMAGINATION

You know what's real. Though you are a quick study, your knowledge is unrehearsed and magical. Most times you don't know how you know what you know. But you do know.

You know a lot. You are a quick study. Most times you don't know how you know what you know. You seem to know everything, or at least have some idea about a wide range of subjects. At its best your knowledge is unrehearsed and magical, otherworldly at times. Your brilliance occurs like a flash of lighting across the midnight mind; it illuminates everything. People around you rely on you for your insight and ability to illuminate complex issues. You know what is real. A word from you is like a reality check. You can see into the heart of a matter. In all this you are aided by your Twin Essence, IMAGI-NATION. Your ability to accept what is imagined as real gives you a firm base for your pronouncements—otherwise known as "your intuition." If you think it, you say it. With you, statements are made as if they are fact. Usually you are correct.

Shadow
The Explainer

Your shadow is triggered by feelings of rejection and stagnation—feeling forced to adhere to the status quo of things. Feeling ashamed, excluded, or being made to look stupid is intolerable for you; when you feel any of these things, you have to prove yourself. In order to feel valuable, you tend to talk a lot and become a bit of a know it all or "smart ass." You are constantly giving reasons for everything, constantly finding the need to explain yourself and your actions to others. You explain away your positions, the reasons for your beliefs, opinions and actions. When talking a lot, you tend not to keep your own counsel and have been known to leak secrets. Alternatively, or in tandem with this, in your attempt to break with the status quo you can also be a prankster/trickster, playing the fool by asking difficult questions to trip people up. You are often called cynical, skeptical, or overly "analytical." Sometimes people may accuse you of not seeing other points of view because you are so busy demonstrating your truth. You can be prone to impatience because, aided by IMAGI-NATION, you have seen the future and it must happen now. The explainer in you wants to be acknowledged as sensible and valuable. You have a strong distrust for those in authority especially if they do not listen to you. You like to have the last word. Often when you are this way your twin, IMAGINATION, is equally triggered, and so may not be as reliable as a basis for your intuition. Your famous last words: "I told you so."

FREEDOM
PLAYFUL · FLOWING

On a River of Movement

NATURE | WATER

Twin Essence ~ COMPASSION

You cannot be pinned down. You come and go as you wish. For you the world is a huge place and life is a playground.

Like a river in its fullness on its way to the sea, you are always on the move. You are like air in that you cannot be pinned down. You come and go as you wish. You go places and do things that other people only dream of. For you, life is a playful game whose objective is to be free to go wherever one pleases, whenever. The people around you are inspired by your ability to move around freely. Like a river, when faced with an obstacle you are undiminished. You can keep moving by breaking yourself off into several different tributaries, only to re-unite again without missing a beat. You are a freewheeler with great flair and a gift for improvisation. Breakdowns and the unexpected energize you, offering an opportunity for new adventure. Aided by your Twin Essence, KINDNESS/INTEGRATION, you are naturally able to blend in; you become part of the mix by feeling out the people around you.

Shadow
The Drifter

Having to be in the same place for a long time is intolerable for you. You are easily bored. You hate to feel like you are spinning your wheels. In order to avoid feeling stagnation and to feel in control you are always on the move. You tend not to identify with any one particular group. You follow your feelings. When you have to go, you move quickly and tend to cut your ties. This can be startling for the people who have come to depend on your free and loving style. Despite being willing to cut your ties you always seem to complain about feeling restricted. You complain that other people and events are restricting your freedom and that having to follow someone else's system irritates you. These complaints are a marvel to the people around you. You say you are still struggling for freedom, yet you appear to be the most free-wheeling person in the world. Usually your friends are in far flung places. People find it hard to get a fix on you. Some complain of feeling abandoned by you. They complain of not being able to keep up with you. It can be a challenge for you to build really lasting friendships or take on long-term business projects or commitments that do not allow for your style. Your famous last words: "I have got to go!"

HARMONY
MELODY-MAKER · HARMONIZER

The Source of Music

NATURE | EARTH

Twin Essence ~ ORDER

Because of you everyone gets along. You like to keep things nice, without you or anyone "sticking out."

You are the music the wind makes as it moves across the earth. Your aim is to keep everyone in your community—be it at work or in the family—moving in the same direction. You are always looking to find the commonalities. Keeping things nice is important. You actively work for the people around you to get along in shared environments and physical spaces. You will always seek to avoid conflict or chaos, to make sure everyone is included and to keep things "nice." You are polite and you give people all the necessary courtesies. You have a faithful ally in your Twin Essence, ORDER. This allows you to have a great appreciation for timing such that you easily make sense of sudden change. Even when things seem chaotic or ill-timed you can make it appear all perfectly orchestrated.

Shadow
Pollyanna

Your shadow is triggered by hopelessness and overwhelming chaos. In the presence of discord and chaos you will sell out your point of view, opinions, and beliefs to fit in. When you are like this you are abandoned by your Twin Essence, ORDER. Your natural ability to make sense of ill-timed events falters. Slowly you tend to lose your voice, your say in how things go. You will do whatever it takes—even deny the facts— to keep a sense of movement and progress since thoughts of hopelessness and stagnation repulse you. You would rather see a glass that is half full as enough for you. Though you usually try hard to keep your contrary feelings to yourself, this has its limits. When the symmetry of your version of the world is interrupted, you will talk negatively about others. You will spread bad news, whispering close to the ground your version of the truth about those "bad" people. This is your way of restoring your sense of control and "harmonious" balance. You won't tell the person to their face, but you will tell others. Speaking your truth out loud is not your style so you are selective with your gossiping. Your famous last words: "Why can't we all just get along?"

DYNAMISM
Charming · Charismatic

The Bright Light at the Center of Things

Mineral | Fire

Twin Essence ~ MYSTERY

Spellbinding, you are a natural charmer, a very bright light. Others are attracted to and inspired by your presence and charm.

You are a natural star. You are a charmer—a very bright light that is always at the center of things. Others are attracted by your natural dynamism and spontaneity. You don't mind being in the spotlight. To see you in action is to be instantly attracted like a fly to a light. You are the great communicator. When you have something to say or an idea to sell people will listen and be sold. You are relied on to inspire. You have the ability to help others see the deepest and best parts of themselves and they see themselves in you. With your Twin Essence, MYSTERY, you often appear unpredictable and awesome—sometimes cloaked and at other times dazzling in your beauty. You have the ability to pull from the unseen and demonstrate in the present what others can only feel. This is what you are loved for.

Shadow
Dazzler

Your shadow is triggered by feelings of shame, rejection, and irrelevance. You do not like feeling that you have disappointed your audience. You do not like feeling embarrassed or like a fraud. Looking good is important to you. When you think you may have let others down you tend to throw "diamonds": make any promise that will seduce, impress, or offer new satisfaction. Anything that makes you look bad is a serious threat to you. For you, image is everything. You will talk a lot to impress. When you break a promise, though late, you will come up with a more dazzling result than the one previously promised, or make a new promise of something even greater. You are generally thought of as charismatic, but unpredictable and unreliable. In rare cases, like dynamite, if ignited, you can be explosive. Depending on your style, your explosion can be masked or bombastic. Others sometimes see you as needing "special attention," as someone who must be "handled with care." For you it's all about impulse. Because of the fast pace of your life, you often forget what was promised, lose track of your promises, feel guilty about it, and end up avoiding the people to whom the promises were made. At other times, you may even try to convince them that what you are delivering is what was promised. You are who we love to hate because when you come through you are spectacular, but when you don't, we can't stand you. Your famous last words: "I will show them."

IMAGINATION
POSSIBLE · POTENTIAL · VISIONARY

All Encompassing Vision

FIRE | MINERAL

Twin Essence ~ WISDOM

You can see possibilities where other people don't. You are not afraid to dream.

The height, breadth, and depth of your world vision is all encompassing. You are able to keep your eyes on many different horizons at the same time. You can see around corners. You look beyond the present circumstances and see great possibilities where others don't. When people feel stuck they rely on you to show them new ways of knowing and experiencing themselves in newer and "realer" ways. You have an ability to reframe things in a way that gives new meaning to the mundane by revealing its potential. With the aid of your Twin Essence, WISDOM, you can easily see beyond the surface of things. You are always looking to sell a new idea, to enroll someone in a new and exciting possibility. You are entranced with the idea of change and transformation. You are change's advocate. You point to the need for it and outline what's possible when people engage difficult changes.

Shadow
The Dreamer

Your shadow is the mask with which you avoid feeing stuck and invisible. You inspire others, yet you confuse them. You can wear them out with your dreaming. Sometimes it may be hard for you to tell the difference between yourself and your dreams. It can be difficult for you to narrow things down because somehow you feel that narrowing your focus diminishes your value. You don't want to feel worthless. When you are trying to justify your existence and feel in control of the movement of things, your imagination tends to go overboard. You seem to have a lot of things going on at any one time and you have difficulty letting go of anything for fear that you will realize you have been standing still and very little has changed. Because of the breadth and depth of your vision, you can be very convincing; however, once bitten by your dreaming, people tend to shy away, refusing to be caught up again in the web of your imagination. With your Twin Essence, WISDOM/INTUITION, also out of balance, the possibilities become endless, literally; yet you insist on the veracity of them all. All your dreams seem so real. Often not much gets done, or things proceed very slowly under the weight of your dreaming. Your famous last words: *"Let's look at it this way..."*

PURITY
SINGLE-MINDED · FOCUSED · PASSIONATE

The Power of Will

FIRE | FIRE

The Pure Essence of FIRE

*You are intentional, clear, and focused. The results of
your single-mindedness are legendary.*

You are the pure essence of fire. You work alone and quickly. Like a
laser beam, you are highly focused. When you set your sights on a
goal you are single minded in your intention to make it real. You play
all the way or not at all. You have a clear list of priorities. The things
you accomplish simply by being single minded over a long period of
time are astounding to others. The people around you rely on you to
provide a perspective that keeps them focused. Your intensity is all
consuming. You are a minimalist. You are known for being efficient
and getting to the point. You can easily see through the superfluous
and burn it away. You can also see clearly through situations and
people. Like a purifying fire, you have the power to reduce everything

to its real meaning and essence and convey that to others.

Shadow
The Zealot

Your shadow is triggered by shame, rejection, feelings of worthless-ness, or inadequacy. When triggered by these feelings your light can often be blinding. Though sometimes inspiring, the purity of your intention and focus can be overwhelming for others. You cannot tol-erate the superfluous or the thought that something might be im-penetrable or unachievable. You set goals in order to give yourself a sense of purpose and accomplishment. You are uncomfortable with being off track or without a specific goal. To avoid feeling this way you will find a goal and become hyper focused, planning and schem-ing a lot, sometimes to the point of isolating yourself from others who are not helpful in the pursuit of your goal. Your intensity is often so strong that you tend to burn others who are less focused or who get in your way. Because of this, others can feel intimidated around you. You can often come off as harsh. When you are this way you are like the sun at high noon: you tend not to see your own shadow or the shadows of others. To others you can seem unfeeling. In extreme cases, you may be accused of zealotry. When you are like this you tend to find refuge in beliefs that you hold very intently and uncom-promisingly. If you turn to religion or spirituality, you will tend to go for extreme expressions of spiritual practice, diet, or religious doc-trine. You lean toward fanaticism and being alone. Your famous last words: "I am burnt out."

CREATIVITY
INNOVATIVE · ORIGINAL · INVENTIVE

New Everyday

FIRE | WATER

Twin Essence ~ CLARITY

The things you express, no one ever has. You are an endless stream of innovation.

You are a generator—a fiery channel through which all things that are new flow into the world. The creations you express, no one ever has before you. You have truly original and bright ideas. Whatever your field, you are a true artist. Because of you the world experiences itself as new every day. You are always at work expanding your self-expression by innovating on what has gone before. You are always willing to take risks, to experience the adventure of something new. You are willing to follow the course of things and to bring different ideas together into a cohesive whole. You use that cohesion to illuminate hidden truths. Working closely with you is your Twin Essence, SIMPLICITY. You can distill and transfigure the soul of things, making them transparent and giving others new eyes through which to easily understand things.

Shadow
The Perfectionist

Your shadow appears when you are hobbled by the insecurity of rejection and the fear of not being valued for your work. When this happens, it is hard for you to see things as complete. You hide behind perfectionism out of fear of rejection. As a result, you are constantly perfecting the product, so much so that it often does not get out. You like your work to look good and you right along with it. You say that you cannot stand the thought of your work looking bad because it is an extension of you. At stake are approval, engagement, and being taken seriously. You often seem to others to be preoccupied with reinventing the wheel. You tend to have very high standards. You often spend a lot of time comparing answers and working for the perfect narrative. When you are like this your unbalanced twin, SIMPLIC-ITY, persuades you that everything is very "complex." You become mired in your work, trying to figure everything out in order to distill it. Sometimes, though not often, you are on the flip side of this: persuaded that everything is so simple, your creations can become too understated and presented in a rush for approval. In this way, you tend to swing between over-preparing the work and sending it too soon to the market. When you appear to be working too hard at it, people around you will often get frustrated with you and not want to work (or even play) with you because you can be so demanding, but you will keep at it. You know the difference your hard work makes, even if they don't. Your famous last words: "I am still working on it!"

STRENGTH
INVINCIBLE · HEROIC

Warrior & Defender

FIRE | EARTH

Twin Essence ~ NURTURING

*You cannot be defeated. People around you rely on you
to do the heavy lifting when things are difficult.*

You are the earthbound quality of FIRE. You are made of the toughest metal tempered in the earth by the fiercest of fires. Though you may not necessarily be a big person physically, you have a lot of energy. This energy—the intensity of your thoughts, words, and actions—is put to work to nurture and protect the things you can see clearly and believe in. You are invincible, so you can cut through anything. People rely on you to do the heavy lifting when things are difficult, to make a way where there is no path. You have strong convictions. Your energy is often used in tandem with your Twin Essence, NURTURING. This has you coming to the defense and protection of the weak and all who come to you for help and shelter.

You are an untiring fighter for the causes you believe in.

Shadow
The Attacker

Your shadow is triggered by rejection, invisibility, and feeling unsafe. You cannot tolerate being unjustly vilified, feeling vulnerable, looking like a failure, or feeling ashamed. Similarly, you do not like the thought that others are weakened or homeless, made to feel ashamed or powerless. You tend to have a problem with people in authority who you think abuse their power. When you feel that you or others are under attack you will attack verbally or physically to defend against the evil intentions, attitudes, and actions of others. When triggered in this way, your attack is often disproportionate to the perceived affront. You will attack with the same methods and tools with which you say you have been attacked. You will mirror the strategy of your perceived attacker. You will paint yourself as the victim and complain bitterly about what others are doing to you. You have the ability to kill others. If you don't kill them physically you can kill them with a look. You are that strong. When you are this way, your Twin Essence, NURTURING, will depart. As NURTURING does in her own imbalanced state, you will practice your own version of "tough love"—kicking ass in service of the people under your protection and the principles you believe in. In this state, you can destroy everything. Nothing will be left standing. Your fighting words: "Don't mess with me!"

SELF-SUFFICIENCY
RESOURCEFUL · INDEPENDENT · SELF-SUSTAINING

The Well That Never Runs Dry

WATER | MINERAL

Twin Essence ~ JOY

You are very resourceful. You will find the means to do whatever is required of you. You will work hard and not ask for help.

Feeling content and having the freedom to speak your mind are very important to you. You are very resourceful and independent. You will find the means to do whatever is required of you or to acquire what you or others need. People rely on you to find a way where there is none. The lengths to which you will go to get what you need are legendary among your friends and family. At your best, you are like a well that never runs dry for anyone. You can bring people together and make the requests necessary to move projects along. When no one else has enough, you do. Because of your Twin Essence, JOY, you always seem pretty content, secure in the idea that you have all that you need or the resources to attain it.

Shadow
The Independent

You are vulnerable to abandonment, betrayal, and the feeling of being unheard. Asking for something and not getting it hurts. You do not like being without or left wanting. When you feel this way, you find yourself always planning for a rainy day or just plain worried about one. Feeling dependent on others is intolerable so when things are difficult you work hard and do not ask for help. In fact, you will not ask for help even if this means having to be in the gutter. You are just too proud to beg. You often have a tendency to hoard things. In extreme cases, though you are not necessarily a thief, you are not beyond pinching stuff from the job or restaurants—things that are "free." What is "free" varies with your feelings of contentment and sufficiency. At times, you will not be truthful about what you have in order to get more. Famous last words: "No, thank you, I am good."

COMPASSION
Kind · Integrating· Empathetic

Feels Everything

Water | Nature

Twin Essence ~ FREEDOM

You are able to feel everything deeply without becoming bitter. Most things leave an impression on you. You are especially kind to strangers and others who are different.

You are like the gently moving water that heals all wounds. You are able to feel deeply the changing fortunes of everyone and everything. People come to you with their troubles because they know you will feel their pain and help them navigate life's changes. You will often spend long hours with people who are suffering, listening to their concerns and tending to their needs. Your caring knows no bounds. Like your Twin Essence, FREEDOM, when necessary you can divide yourself into many different pieces to satisfy all the demands made of you. It is easy for you to put yourself in another's shoes. You are especially kind to strangers and others who are different or seen as outcasts. You do not like feeling that you or anyone has been abandoned or is lonely. When you notice that people feel this way your heart bleeds.

Shadow
Bleeding Heart

To avoid feeling alone and hopeless, you will lose yourself in the concerns of others. When this happens your pain and that of others become one. Seemingly small things can be very painful for you. You often feel paralyzed and alienated. When you feel like this, stuff doesn't get done. You seem unable to be truthful about your own pain and boundaries. You often care beyond what is prudent. Your family members and close friends, whose pain is less obvious than the people you help, complain that they cannot get your attention. Because you are so busy caring for others they often feel abandoned, neglected, and uncared for. You often complain that people take advantage of your kindness, yet you struggle to allow yourself to receive from others. Famous first words: "How are you feeling?"

SIMPLICITY
CLEAR · AUTHENTIC

Transparent & Uncomplicated

WATER | FIRE

Twin Essence ~ CREATIVITY

You see truth as beauty. You are transparent—nothing is hidden. Deceptive in your simplicity, you have the ability to break down complexity and the seemingly intractable.

You see truth as beauty. You like to keep things authentic and unadorned. You are able to see and accept things as they really are—to make sense of seeming differences and find the common denominator. You can see through things clearly. Very little is really complicated to you. You can be trusted to say it like it is. The people around you rely on you to give them your opinion directly. Though they may not like your opinion, they are confident it is yours and it can clear up a lot of nonsense. You like to clarify things and get to the bottom line. You like everything to be laid out on the table and up front so that you know what you are dealing with. Like your twin, CREA-TIVITY, you have a strong drive to get to the soul of things. It is your clarity and directness that solve seemingly complex riddles, causing everyone to see.

Shadow
The Bottom Line

You struggle with abandonment and rejection. You like being authentic and connected so you do not like lies or complications of any kind. When looking good is in jeopardy you will tend to oversimplify things to yourself and others. When you think that the truth may be too complex or lead to conflict, you will often not say your true feelings. You prefer to misrepresent or trivialize the facts about what really happened or your point of view in order to cast yourself in a more positive light. You want to be known for your clarity so you will oversimplify your truth or come to a too pat conclusion. On the other hand, there are times when you make things just too complicated and like your twin, CREATIVITY, spend an inordinate amount of time to get to your brand of perfection: the truth. You tend to keep things neat and moving along even if they are dirty. When you are in avoidance mode you will just not say anything. You will take things and people at face value, not probing beneath the surface. As a result, you can miss details in things and the character flaws of others. Some people may lie to you. Others will accuse you (and you will accuse yourself) of being gullible or naive.

RELATIONSHIP
Intimate · Connected · Networked

Infinite Correlation

Water | Water

Pure Essence of WATER

You are easily drawn to people. You are keenly aware of everyone's interconnection. You keep everyone in touch.

You have a great sense of being related with everyone. You are naturally drawn to people and are keenly aware of everyone's interconnectedness. You are a great networker. People rely on you to bring them together. You constantly and easily fall in love with everyone. You move easily among people at gatherings. People do not scare you; you are turned on by them in larger numbers than most people. Nothing would give you greater joy than to get everyone talking to each other and connecting. You are the first person to try to iron out a conflict between your friends.

Shadow
The Needy

You are vulnerable to betrayal, abandonment, and loneliness. Though you love people you are afraid that they will hurt you, so you often operate as a "lone" ranger. More so than others, you have a great fear of this isolation. You want to feel accepted and included. You crave deep relationships and intimacy. When this is not met, you can be needy and jealous. You have lots of potential relationships (because you seldom permanently break ties), but because of your fear of abandonment you tend not to commit on the one hand, or commit too easily on the other. You can bring the party together, but you leave bored. You tend to push people away when things get "too good." The people who love you never seem to know if you are coming or going.

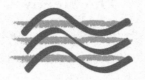

ORGANIZATION
FLOWING · COORDINATED · PATTERNED

The Organizer

WATER | EARTH

Twin Essence ~ NOURISHMENT

You make things flow effortlessly. You know which things belong together and where they should be placed. You can see patterns and trends. You can plan anything down to the last detail.

You make things flow. Because of you everything and everyone are kept on track. If you were not around, things and people would collide. You know what belongs together and where they should be placed. You can see patterns and trends. If you don't you will create them. You can plan anything down to the last detail. People around you rely on your strategic thinking, your ability to track best and worst case scenarios, to see the bigger picture, and all of the steps in between. It is you who keeps things on their track.

Shadow
The Control Freak

Because of your fear of abandonment and instability you can be controlling. You do not feel safe until you are sure that everything is planned for. When these stressors are in play, you tend to defend yourself against things that are different and which make you uncomfortable. You do not believe that things will "fall into place." You like it when things that belong together stay together. You constantly complain that other people do not know what they are doing. You don't want to be a part of anything that looks chaotic and you are the only one responsible. No one knows except you because you can see how it all fits together. If things do not happen "right" this could reflect on you, so you take care of things yourself. You are sometimes called a "control freak." People may have difficulty working with you because you tend to be a micromanager and this can be disempowering. Having to do it all yourself can be stressful.

POWER

Masterful · Accountable · Able

The Authority

Earth | Mineral

Twin Essence ~ PATIENCE

You are naturally able to get the job done exceptionally well. You have the ability to move mountains. The buck stops with you. You know where things are and you are highly influential over great distances.

You are like Everest, a high mountain resting on a great stone deeply embedded comfortably in the earth. You are highly eloquent and influential over great distances. You are the authority in your field. From where you sit you have the big picture and big thoughts to match. You are naturally able to get the job done by speaking powerfully while taking care of the people around you—for you can see them clearly. You do things that seem impossible to others. The buck stops with you. You are accountable. You know where all the beans are. Your reach and insight are all encompassing. Your Twin Essence, PATIENCE, gives you support by telling you when to act and when to wait for things to unfold. Whether your style is passive or aggressive, subtle or overt, it is you who can move the mountain.

Shadow
The Abuser

Your shadow is triggered by the fear of feeling vulnerable, irrelevant, or silenced in any way. The dilemmas in which these feelings arise are intolerable. These are times when answers are not easy to find and your sense of security is threatened by the chaos around you. To avoid self-doubt and to feel secure, you will say that you don't have any power and retreat into silence or give away your power, only to start speaking up and taking action suddenly when irrelevance threatens. When you do this, others experience you like an avalanche. Where care is to be taken, you will have none. Your natural ability to influence will give way to what may be considered abusive words and actions. When triggered in this way you complain that others are not up to the job or are not giving you your due respect. You tend to set impossibly high and specific standards of behavior for yourself and others. When you let yourself down you will feel guilty, but you will tend to cover it up. On the other hand, you will often call down public retribution on others who do not meet your standards. When you are this way you have left the counsel of your Twin Essence, PATIENCE, so your sense of restfulness and self-confidence fail you and are replaced by a restless energy that's like a wrecking ball. Your famous last words: "Respect me!"

ORDER
Consistent · Disciplined · Persistent

The Rhythm of Life

Earth | Nature

Twin Essence ~ HARMONY

*You are reliable, disciplined, and consistent. You have
a heightened awareness of timing and rhythm.*

You have regular, persistent actions and habits and you will keep at
things until they get done. You are the energy that fuels the change
of seasons. You are a very reliable and disciplined person. Because
you are this way you thrive on a sense of certainty, consistency and
safety. Everyone relies on you for a sense of rhythm. You are able to
devise both simple and more complex rhythms. You have a strong
relationship with time, but not time in the conventional sense of a
steady beat, necessarily. Things can be out of what some would consider a "regular rhythm" and this would be okay for you. You are able
to decipher the unique timing and sequence of things. Things that
seemingly appear from out of the blue do not throw you because you

have a way—a point of view—with which to see and place the unexpected. You have a place for them. You can easily bring a sense of order to what others see as chaotic. You have a strong relationship with your Twin Essence, HARMONY. She helps you hear rhythms and sequences that others don't so that you know when to act and when it is best not to.

Shadow
The Task Master

Your shadow is triggered by feelings of chaos—a sudden loss of security and a sense of things being hopeless or out of control. Though you work for change you do not like when it comes too suddenly or is disorderly in ways that threaten your established identity. Being out of time and rhythm is upsetting and disorienting for you. To avoid feeling this way and to feel in control you will insist on your own way. In the process, you will blow away people who get in the way. You are not turned around easily. When you are like this you tend to stick to your point of view and actions regardless of the consequences. When under stress you seem to spend very little time reflecting on the consequences of your actions. When upset you will often claim to be under the order, authority, and power of someone else and will follow those orders to the letter. You will maintain the status quo. Though you are dependable you tend to be anal about rules, regulations, and procedures. You can be stubborn about policies and practices and seldom change them to accommodate anyone. When you are out of balance in this way, you are not synced with your Twin Essence, HARMONY. In this way, HARMONY is not listening for the syncopated rhythms and timing that tell it when to act. Things become very linear and one dimensional such that there is a chronological and linear sequencing of things, a steady regular beat and sense of monotony that is relied upon to protect you against feelings of being lost and vulnerable. Your famous last words: "It's time."

NURTURING
WARM · EVOLUTIONARY · CATALYZING

The Motivator

EARTH | FIRE

Twin Essence ~ STRENGTH

Because of your warmth and protection, the people and things around you grow and flourish.

Because of your warmth and comfort, the things and people around you grow and flourish. You love to support the growth and development of others. You are a natural nurturer and you are constantly growing yourself. You are often the adviser, confidant, and motivator. You are relied on for your insight and ability to keep spaces safe for the people around you. You are like the warm bosom of the earth. You can bring stability to chaotic situations by quickly seeing what's missing and easily providing it. Folks love to gather around you. Your presence is in high demand by people who long to be truly seen and to feel a sense of home and belonging. You can totally relate to them—the outcast and the unvalued—because you have been there.

Aided by your Twin Essence, STRENGTH, the love you offer is strong, secure, and grounding.

Shadow
The Martyr

Your shadow is triggered by feelings of dislocation and rejection. When you crave belonging and to be valued you will take care of everyone and not take care of yourself. Often when you are this way the advice and help you give are unsolicited. You will tend to neglect yourself, your health, and finances and leave your own well-being to others. You think that they will take care of you out of pity or guilt because you have done so much for others and are so valuable. When they do not take care of you, your world is wrecked. You are like a man walking in front of moving cars thinking they will not hit him, but when they do, he wonders why? You seem not to value your own life. When you make requests of others for help, often those requests are so great that no one can fill them, so you complain about not having the help you need or that no one is taking care of you. Your giving becomes a game of tit for tat. When you are like this your Twin Essence, STRENGTH, which is also imbalanced, comes to help you out. This can send you to the opposite side of your imbalance, where you practice your unique version of tough love: attacking, withholding, and defending yourself against those who have mistreated you.

NOURISHING
RICH · GENEROUS · GIVING

The Rain Maker

EARTH | WATER

Twin Essence ~ RELATIONSHIP

You are like a mother's milk. You give to people joy-fully exactly what they need, even if their need is un-spoken. And you do so without thinking about the lim-its of your own resources, be they large or small.

You give generously to people exactly what they need, even if their need is unspoken. You have many children who love to suckle. You are a provider who does this without thinking about the limits of your own resources, be they large or small. You are rich in partnerships, relationships, and a sense of family. You have a great thirst for personal fulfillment, happiness, and satisfaction for everyone. The thought that someone is without and in danger is intolerable to you. You hate a vacuum so you will always seek to fill space by giving. You give not only money, but also supportive words and gifts. Aided by your Twin Essence, ORGANIZATION, you want to keep things moving along, around whatever obstacles might arise.

Shadow
Milk Money

Your shadow is triggered by a sense of abandonment, betrayal, and a sense of un-fairness or jeopardy. When under stress you rely on your ability to give in order to be included by others and to include others whose viability is threatened. When this happens, you may give outrageously and unwisely. As you discover that your giving does not always result in feeling accepted or make you immune from attack— and it usually does not, especially in cases where being included or accepted has become critical for you—you can become cynical, bitter, and just plain confused about life and your place in it. This can result in more wanton spending and indulgences on yourself and others who latch on to you for the milk money you offer. When you see this happening, you may strike out by cutting off the people you once nourished with gifts and support. You will become rigid and cold and guard your personal space zealously. Loss of a personal sense of self and the feeling that you are drowning in meaningless "stuff" can be the result. Your famous last words: "What do you need?"

BALANCE
Stable · Grounded · Just

The Ground

Earth | Earth

Pure Essence of EARTH

You are a protector with an innate sense of fairness. You can see both sides of things very clearly without having the need to take either side. You are only interested in what's right.

You are the pure essence of earth. You enjoy creating spaces where everyone can gather and have a sense of belonging. You see yourself as the protector of your community and its spaces —its sacredness and safety. You have a natural sense of fairness and graciousness. You can see both sides of things clearly without having to take either side. People want to have you around in a dispute as you seldom let allegiances or friendships get in the way of how you see things. You are often fun to be with and folks tend to gather around. Your presence naturally generates a feeling of home. People like your impartial, grounded, and easy-going manner. You will always do the right thing.

Shadow
Blind Crusader

Your shadow is triggered by feelings of chaos—a sense of being vulnerable to invasion, attack, and grave injustice. Because you have a strong sense of being the keeper of community you have no tolerance for watching as you and others are treated badly. This is especially true the more you identify with the victim or relate personally to the injustice or violation. This can cut you too close to the bone and often turns you into a blind crusader for justice. When things are getting out of control and your sense of your world as a safe place is threatened, you can become a rigid arbitrator of wrongs and rights. You will tend to insist on things being black or white. You can be a final and unforgiving judge who seldom budges from her position once judgment is dispensed. People call you at your worst, "inflexible." When you are like this you are seen to walk with a big stick. People walk quietly around you because your brand of justice is dispensed recklessly regardless of the consequences of your actions on the guilty or the innocent. Your famous last words: "That's not right!"

Recommended Reading

Malidoma Patrice Some

Of Water & The Spirit

The Healing Wisdom of Africa

Ritual

Deepak Chopra

Creating Affluence

Eckhart Tolle

Stillness Speaks

The Power of Now

A New Earth

Michael Bernard Beckwith

Life Visioning

Pierluigi Confalonieri

The Clock of Vipassana Has Struck

Maharishi Mahesh Yogi
The Science of Being and the Art of Living

Paramahansa Yogananda
The Autobiography of a Yogi

John Ruskan
Emotional Clearing

Robert Moore & Douglas Gillette
King, Warrior, Magician, Lover

Swami Muktananda
The Play of consciousness - An Spiritual Autobiography

Next Steps

If you have enjoyed this book here are some next steps for you.

1.
Join The Community

Join the community of fellow BLOOMERS and get early access to upcoming books. Visit our websites and follow us on social media for additional resources and support for your journey.

WEBSITES

www.theessentialjourney.com

www.thebloombooks.com

www.olubode.com

FACEBOOK

Group: BLOOM The Essential Journey

Page: BLOOM The Essential Journey

INSTAGRAM

@bloomtheessentialjourney

@olubode

HASHTAGS

#bloomtheessentialjourney #thebloombook #olubode

TWITTER

olubodeshawnb

2
Subscribe To The Inbloom Podcast

In BLOOM is produced for and features BLOOMers – ordinary people who are doing extra-ordinary things by leveraging their talents, skills and resources in order to create new ways of living and being for their own survival. This podcast seeks to inspire and inform listeners who are trying to figure out their own lives and deliver their gifts for the world. Available on iTunes

3
Share This Book

Please write a review on Amazon and tell others who you think will enjoy this book. Spreading the word helps to reach new readers, grow this movement and continue putting out similar content.

THANK YOU

ABOUT THE AUTHOR

Olubode Shawn Brown was born in Jamaica where he spent the formative years of his life until young adulthood. He grew up in Jamaica's churches. As a young man who knew that he was gay, he was completely surrounded by fixed religious and cultural ideas of what was right and what was wrong. Yet from boyhood he has been in search of "unseen things." After graduating from law school, he left Jamaica for the United States and has since worked as an attorney, corporate consultant, artist-advisor, and life coach in Los Angeles and New York City.

A year after he arrived in New York City the AIDS epidemic hit like a slowly exploding bomb, and many of the young men who had become his brothers began to die. The trauma of it all shook him to the core. His world fell apart. America had become a nightmare. This launched him on a journey to recapture faith and to find what really matters.

On this journey with many teachers and guides, he has experienced a series of profound insights that have radically changed his life. He works now as an artist and facilitator devoted to celebrating the freedom of these insights and sharing his journey with others.

His work synergizes and reflects the timeless wisdom of the Dagara people of West Africa and the Vedic seers of India. He fuses this wisdom with the distinctions of transformation, emotional intelligence, and the teachings of the great metaphysicians of our time. His simple distillation of these truths uses the elements of mineral, nature, fire, water, and earth as metaphors to help reveal an exciting new paradigm of life balance, to help us each understand our unique inner pathways to personal growth, and to help us realize the possibility and urgency of delivering our life's gifts.

Olubode lives in New York City where he produces events, media, and travel experiences that introduce his core philosophy to a global audience. He is the founder and facilitator of a global community called BLOOM.